Michelle

English
Assignments 1
NEW EDITION

Brian A Lenehan

THE EDUCATIONAL COMPANY

First published 1█████

The Educational Company Of Ireland
Ballymount Road
Walkinstown
Dublin 12

The paper used in this book comes from Managed Forests in Northern Europe For every tree felled, at least one new tree is planted

Approved Quality System

A Trading Unit of Smurfit Services Limited

© Brian A. Lenehan 1995

Design and Artwork: Design Image
Cover design: Design Image
Printed in the Republic of Ireland by Smurfit Print

AEN 5101 S – 0123456789

■ ACKNOWLEDGMENTS

The publishers wish to acknowledge the following for permission to reproduce copyright material: The Irish Times; Peters Fraser & Dunlop for *Janey Mary* by James Plunkett; The Society of Authors for *London Spring 1941* by Eiluned Lewis; Rogers, Coleridge & White Ltd. for *The Confessional* by Seán O' Faoláin; Jonathan Cape Ltd. for *The Wild Duck's Nest* by Michael McLaverty; Hutchinson Publishing Group Ltd. for *The Confirmation Suit* by Brendan Behan; Jonathan Cape Ltd. and Penguin Books Ltd., for *The Hitch-hiker* by Roald Dahl from *The Wonderful Story of Henry Sugar*; Peters Frazer Dunlop Group Ltd. for an extract from *The Boy on the Capstan* by James Plunkett; Longman Ltd. for *The Weaker Sex* by Wendy Richmond, *Your Attention Please!* by Peter Porter, *An Introduction to Dogs* by Ogden Nash, *The Song of the Battery Hen* by Edwin Brock, *Digging* by Seamas Heaney, and for an extract from *Cider With Rosie* by Laurie Lee; Cambridge Educational Press for *Cold Feet* by Brian Lee; J.M. Dent and Sons for *Sunset Poem* by Dylan Thomas; Jennifer Johnston and Grafton Books for *Trio* from Best Irish Short Stories 2.

The publishers have made every effort to trace and correctly acknowledge copyright holders. If, however, they have inadvertently overlooked any, they will be pleased to make the necessary arrangements at the earliest opportunity.

CONTENTS

DRAMA EXTRACTS

UNITS 15-18   140 - 163

Prose extracts
Poetry
Media Studies: Advertising and Photography
Personal and Functional writing
Grammar
Composition topics
General questions

UNIT 19

UNIT 20

UNIT 21

Prose extracts and poetry include pieces by Alice E. Chase,
Wendy Richmond, Edmund Hillary, Louise Andrews Kent, Ogden Nash,
Rosemary Sutcliff, James Vance Marshall, Laurie Lee, Dylan Thomas,
Desmond Bagley, Patrick Kavanagh and W.B. Yeats.

SHORT STORIES

➤ The Confirmation Suit

BRENDAN BEHAN

For weeks it was nothing but simony and sacrilege, and the sins crying to heaven for vengeance, the big green Catechism in our hands, walking home along the North Circular Road. And after tea, at the back of the brewery wall, with a butt too, to help our wits, what is a pure spirit, and don't kill that, Billser has to get a drag out of it yet. What do I mean by apostate, and hell and heaven and despair and presumption and hope? The big fellows, who were now thirteen and the veterans of last year's Confirmation, frightened us, and said the Bishop would fire us out of the chapel if we didn't answer his questions, and we'd be left wandering around the streets, in a new suit and top-coat with nothing to show for it, all dressed up and nowhere to go. The big people said not to mind them; they were only getting it up for us, jealous because they were over their Confirmation, and could never make it again. At school we were in a special room to ourselves, for the last few days, and went round, a special class of people. There were worrying times too, that the Bishop would light on you, and you wouldn't be able to answer his questions. Or you might hear the women complaining about the price of boys' clothes.

'Twenty-two and sixpence for tweed, I'd expect a share in the shop for that. I've a good mind to let him go in jersey and pants for that.'

'Quite right, ma'am,' says one to another, backing one another up, 'I always say what matter if they are good and pure.' What had that got to do with it, if you had to go into the Chapel in a jersey and pants, and every other kid in a new suit, kid gloves and tan shoes and a scoil cap. The Cowan brothers were terrified. They were twins, and twelve years old, and every one in the street seemed to be wishing a jersey and pants on them, and saying their poor mother couldn't be expected to do for two in the one year, and she ought to go down to Sister Monica and tell her to put one back. If it came to that, the Cowans agreed to fight it out, at the back of the brewery wall, whoever got best, the other would be put back.

I wasn't so worried about this. My old fellow was a tradesman, and made money most of the time. Besides, my grandmother, who lived at the top of the next house, was a lady of capernosity and function. She had money and lay in

1
▼

bed all day, drinking porter or malt, and taking pinches of snuff, and talking to the neighbours that would call up to tell her the news of the day. She only left her bed to go down one flight of stairs and visit the lady in the back drawing-room, Miss McCann.

Miss McCann worked a sewing-machine, making habits for the dead. Sometimes girls from our quarter got her to make dresses and costumes, but mostly she stuck to the habits. They were a steady line, she said, and you didn't have to be always buying patterns, for the fashions didn't change, not even from summer to winter. They were like a long brown shirt, and a hood attached, that was closed over the person's face before the coffin lid was screwn down. A sort of little banner hung out of one arm, made of the same material, and four silk rosettes in each corner, and in the middle, the letters I.H.S., which mean, Miss McCann said: 'I have Suffered.'

My grandmother and Miss McCann liked me more than any other kid they knew. I liked being liked, and could only admire their taste.

My Aunt Jack, who was my father's aunt as well as mine, sometimes came down from where she lived, up near the Basin, where the water came from before they started getting it from Wicklow. My Aunt Jack said it was much better water, at that. Miss McCann said she ought to be a good judge. For Aunt Jack was funny. She didn't drink porter or malt, or take snuff, and my father said she never thought much about men, either. She was also very strict about washing yourself very often. My grandmother took a bath every year, whether she was dirty or not, but she was in no way bigoted in the washing line in between times.

Aunt Jack made terrible raids on us now and again, to stop snuff and drink, and make my grandmother get up in the morning, and wash herself, and cook meals and take food with them. My grandmother was a gilder by trade, and served her time in one of the best shops in the city, and was getting a man's wages at sixteen. She liked stuff out of the pork butchers, and out of cans, but didn't like boiling potatoes, for she said she was no skivvy, and the chip man was better at it. When she was left alone it was a pleasure to eat with her. She always had cans of lovely things and spicy meat and brawn, and plenty of seasoning, fresh out of the German man's shop up the road. But after a visit from Aunt Jack, she would have to get up and wash for a week, and she would have to go and make stews and boil cabbage and pig's cheeks. Aunt Jack was very much up for sheep's heads, too. They were so cheap and nourishing.

But my grandmother only tried it once. She had been a first-class gilder in Eustace Street, but never had anything to do with sheep's heads before. When she took it out of the pot, and laid it on the plate, she and I sat looking at it, in fear and trembling. It was bad enough going into the pot, but with the soup streaming from its eyes, and its big teeth clenched in a very bad temper, it would put the heart crossways in you. My grandmother asked me, in a whisper, if I ever thought sheep could look so vindictive, but that it was more like the head of an old man, and would I for God's sake take it up and throw it out of the window. The sheep kept glaring at us, but I came the far side of it, and rushed over to the window and threw it out in a flash. My grandmother had to drink a Baby Power whiskey, for she wasn't the better of herself.

Afterwards she kept what she called her stock-pot on the gas. A heap of bones, and as she said herself, any old muck that would come in handy, to have boiling there, night and day, on a glimmer. She and I ate happily of cooked ham and California pineapple and sock-eye salmon, and the pot of good nourishing soup was always on the gas even if Aunt Jack came down the chimney, like the Holy Souls at midnight. My grandmother said she didn't begrudge the money for the gas. Not when she remembered the looks that sheep's head was giving her. And all she had to do with the stock-pot was to throw in another sup of water, now and again, and a handful of old rubbish the pork butcher would send over, in the way of lights or bones. My Aunt Jack thought a lot about barley, too, so we had a package of that lying beside the gas, and threw a sprinkle in any time her foot was heard on the stairs. The stock-pot bubbled away on the gas for years after, and only when my grandmother was dead did someone notice it. They tasted it, and spat it out just as quick, and wondered what it was. Some said it was paste, and more that it was gold size, and there were other people and they maintained that it was glue. They all agreed on one thing, that it was dangerous tack to leave lying around, where there might be young children, and in the heel of the reel, it went out the same window as the sheep's head.

Miss McCann told my grandmother not to mind Aunt Jack but to sleep as long as she liked in the morning. They came to an arrangement that Miss McCann would cover the landing and keep an eye out. She would call Aunt Jack in for a minute, and give the signal by banging the grate, letting on to poke the fire, and have a bit of a conversation with Aunt Jack about dresses and costumes, and hats and habits. One of these mornings, and Miss McCann delaying a fighting action, to give my grandmother time to hurl herself out of bed and into her clothes and give her face the rub of a towel, the chat between Miss McCann and Aunt Jack came to my Confirmation suit.

When I made my first Communion, my grandmother dug deep under the mattress, and myself and Aunt Jack were sent round expensive shops, and I came back with a rig that would take the sight of your eye. This time, however, Miss McCann said there wasn't much stirring in the habit line, on account of the mild winter, and she would be delighted to make the suit, if Aunt Jack would get the material. I nearly wept, for terror of what these old women would have me got up in, but I had to let on to be delighted, Miss McCann was so set on it. She asked Aunt Jack did she remember my father's Confirmation suit. He did. He said he would never forget it. They sent him out in a velvet

3

suit, of plum colour, with a lace collar. My blood ran cold when he told me.

The stuff they got for my suit was blue serge, and that was not so bad. They got as far as the pants, and that passed off very civil. You can't do much to a boy's pants, one pair is like the next, though I had to ask them not to trouble themselves putting three little buttons on either side of the legs. The waistcoat was all right, and anyway the coat would cover it. But the coat itself, that was where Aughrim was lost.

The lapels were little wee things, like what you'd see in pictures like *Ring* magazine of John L. Sullivan, or Gentleman Jim, and the buttons were the size of saucers, or within the bawl of an ass of it, and I nearly cried when I saw them being put on, and ran down to my mother, and begged her to get me any sort of a suit, even a jersey and pants, than have me set up before the people in this get-up. My mother said it was very kind of Aunt Jack and Miss McCann to go to all this trouble and expense, and I was very ungrateful not to appreciate it. My father said that Miss McCann was such a good tailor that people were dying to get into her creations, and her handiwork was to be found in all the best cemeteries. He laughed himself sick at this, and said if it was good enough for him to be sent down to North William Street in plum-coloured velvet and lace, I needn't be getting the needle over a couple of big buttons and little lapels. He asked me not to forget to get up early the morning of my Confirmation, and let him see me, before he went to work: a bit of a laugh started the day well. My mother told him to give over and let me alone, and said she was sure it would be a lovely suit, and that Aunt Jack would never buy poor material, but stuff that would last forever. That nearly finished me altogether, and I ran through the hall up to the corner, fit to cry my eyes out, only I wasn't much of a hand at crying. I went more for cursing, and I cursed all belonging to me, and was hard at it on my father, and wondering why his lace collar hadn't choked him, when I remembered that it was a sin to go on like that, and I going up for Confirmation, and I had to simmer down, and live in fear of the day I'd put on that jacket.

The days passed, and I was fitted and refitted, and every old one in the house came up to look at the suit, and took a pinch of snuff, and a sup out of the jug, and wished me long life and the health to wear and tear it, and they spent that much time viewing it round, back, belly and sides, that Miss McCann hadn't time to make the overcoat, and like an answer to a prayer, I was brought down to Talbot Street, and dressed out in a dinging overcoat, belted, like a grown-up man's. And my shoes and gloves were dear and dandy, and I said to myself that there was no need to let anyone see the suit with its little lapels and big buttons. I could keep the topcoat on all day, in the chapel, and going round afterwards.

The night before Confirmation day, Miss McCann handed over the suit to my mother, and kissed me, and said not to bother thanking her. She would do more than that for me, and she and my grandmother cried and had a drink on the strength of my having grown to be a big fellow, in the space of twelve years, which they didn't seem to consider a great deal of time. My father said to my mother, and I getting bathed before the fire, that since I was born Miss

McCann thought the world of me. When my mother was in hospital, she took me into her place till my mother came out, and it near broke her heart to give me back.

In the morning I got up, and Mrs. Rooney in the next room shouted in to my mother that her Liam was still stalling, and not making any move to get out of it, and she thought she was cursed; Christmas or Easter, Communion or Confirmation, it would drive a body into Riddleys, which is the mad part of Grangegorman, and she wondered she wasn't driven out of her mind, and above in the puzzle factory years ago. So she shouted again at Liam to get up, and washed and dressed. And my mother shouted at me, though I was already knotting my tie, but you might as well be out of the world, as out of fashion, and they kept it up like a pair of mad women, until at last Liam and I were ready and he came in to show my mother his clothes. She handselled him a tanner, which he put in his pocket and Mrs. Rooney called me in to show her my clothes. I just stood at her door, and didn't open my coat, but just grabbed the sixpence out of her hand, and ran up the stairs like the hammers of hell. She shouted at me to hold on a minute, she hadn't seen my suit, but I muttered something about it not being lucky to keep a Bishop waiting, and ran on.

The Church was crowded, boys on one side and the girls on the other, and the altar ablaze with lights and flowers, and a throne for the bishop to sit on when he wasn't confirming. There was a cheering crowd outside, drums rolled, trumpeters from Jim Larkin's band sounded the Salute. The bishop came in and the door was shut. In short order I joined the queue to the rails, knelt and was whispered over, and touched on the cheek. I had my overcoat on the whole time, though it was warm, and I was in a lather of sweat waiting for the hymns and the sermon.

The lights grew brighter and I got warmer, was carried out fainting. But though I didn't mind them loosening my tie, I clenched firmly my overcoat, and nobody saw the jacket with the big buttons and the little lapels. When I went home, I got into bed, and my father said I went into a sickness just as the bishop was giving us the pledge. He said this was a master stroke, and showed real presence of mind.

Sunday after Sunday, my mother fought over the suit. She said I was a liar and a hypocrite, putting it on for a few minutes every week, and running into Miss McCann's and out again, letting her think I wore it every week-end. In a passionate temper my mother said she would show me up, and tell Miss McCann, and up like a shot with her, for my mother was always slim, and light on her feet as a feather, and in next door. When she came back she said nothing, but sat at the fire looking into it. I didn't really believe she would tell Miss McCann. And I put on the suit and thought I would go in and tell her I was wearing it this week-night, because I was going to the Queen's with my brothers. I ran next door and upstairs and every step was more certain and easy that my mother hadn't told her. I ran, shoved in the door, saying: 'Miss Mc., Miss Mc., Rory and Sean and I are going to the Queen's...' She was bent over the sewing-machine and all I could see was the top of her old grey head, and the rest of her shaking with crying, and her arms folded under her head, on a bit of habit where she had been finishing the I.H.S. I ran down the stairs and back into our place, and my mother was sitting at the fire, sad and sorry, but saying nothing.

I needn't have worried about the suit lasting forever. Miss McCann didn't. The next winter was not so mild, and she was whipped before the year was out. At her wake people said how she has in a habit of her own making, and my father said she would look queer in anything else, seeing as she supplied the dead of the whole quarter for forty years, without one complaint from a customer.

At the funeral, I left my topcoat in the carriage and got out and walked in the spills of rain after her coffin. People said I would get my end, but I went on till we reached the graveside, and I stood in my Confirmation suit drenched to the skin. I thought this was the least I cold do.

Brendan Behan's Island

uestions

1 Explain why Brendan dreaded wearing the suit on his Confirmation day. Has it anything to do with the type of boy he was?

2 Was Brendan unfair to Miss McCann? His mother called him 'a liar and a hypocrite'. What do you think?

3 Brendan tried to make up for his actions. How did he attempt to do this?

4 From the evidence of the story, what type of woman do you imagine Miss McCann to have been?

5 Brendan's parents are very different from one another in character and attitude. In what ways is this statement true?

6 Did Brendan's mother make the right decision when she told Miss McCann how he felt about the suit? Support your answer by reference to the story.

7 How would you describe the language used in the story? Explain your answer.

8 Conflict plays an important part in this story. What does it contribute to the overall effect of the story?

➤ Blubber

JUDY BLUME

At eleven Mr Kubeck, the custodian, delivers our lunch milk. He leaves it outside the classroom door, in the hall. When I see it standing there my stomach growls and I start thinking about my peanut-butter sandwich, sitting inside my stuffy old locker, getting soggy. By lunchtime the milk is warm. I think it's sour too. I've told my mother to report that to the Board of Health. We'll be able to buy cold milk next year, when the school gym is converted into a part-time cafeteria. Until then we have to suffer through lunch in our classrooms.

At noon Mrs Minish leaves the room. She goes out to lunch every day. All the teachers do. It makes me mad to think of them sitting in some nice restaurant eating hamburgers and french fries while I have to sit at my desk drinking sour milk.

As soon as Mrs Minish is gone we all move our desks around. I push mine next to Wendy's. So does Caroline. Sometimes Donna Davidson joins us and other times she sits across the room with Laurie, which is fine with me. I can't stand hearing her horse stories.

Linda Fischer eats by herself. I watched as she unpacked her lunch and spread it out across her desk. She had a sandwich, a pack of Hostess cupcakes and a big red apple. 'You're going to turn into a real whale if you keep eating like that,' Wendy told her.

'Just shut up,' Linda said, more to her sandwich than to Wendy.

'Well listen to that!' I said. 'Blubber told Wendy to shut up. Can you imagine!'

'Some people don't know how to talk nice,' Caroline said.

'Didn't your mother teach you any manners, Blubber?' Wendy asked.

'I don't think so,' I said. 'Otherwise Blubber wouldn't chew with her mouth open.'

'Oh yes,' Wendy said. 'I noticed that too. She must want us to see that she has an egg-salad sandwich.'

'On wholewheat bread,' Caroline added.

'And how lovely it looks all chewed up in her mouth,' I said. 'I guess that's why she decided to report on the whale. She has a lot in common with them.' I was beginning to enjoy myself.

'Blub...blub...blub...' Wendy made this funny noise.

Linda took her cupcakes and stuffed them back into her lunch bag. She stood up and headed for the trash basket but Wendy stopped her before she could throw anything away. 'You can't waste those *beautiful* cupcakes, Blubber!'

'I'll take them,' Robby Winters called. Wendy grabbed the bag out of Linda's hand, took out the package of cupcakes and threw it across the room to Robby. He tossed it to Bill, who passed it to Michael. Michael ate one. The other cupcake was squashed by that time but Irwin stuffed it into his mouth anyway.

Linda went back to her desk. Wendy followed her. 'Oh look ... Blubber has a shiny red apple.' She held it up for the class to see. Then she put the apple on top of her head and paraded around the room.

Michael stood on his desk and yelled, 'I'm William Tell!'

'Who's he?' Laurie asked.

'The guy who shot the apple off his kid's head, dummy.' Michael pretended to pull back his bow and aim an arrow at Wendy's head.

'Help ... oh help!' Wendy cried, racing around the room, holding the apple on her head with one hand. 'Help is on the way,' I called, taking off my shoe and throwing it at Michael. It hit him in the leg. He picked it up and ran to the window. 'You wouldn't!' I yelled.

As soon as I said that, Michael raised the windows and tossed out my shoe. It landed in the bushes.

'You jerk!' You absolute idiot!'

'I'll fix him, Jill,' Wendy called, firing the apple at Michael. It missed him and crashed against the blackboard. Bruce picked it up, polished it off on his shirt, then took a bite.

Donna pointed at him and chanted, 'He ate the poison apple...he ate the poison apple...'

'Oh...' Bruce made this gurgling noise, clutched his stomach and dropped to the floor. He rolled over and played dead while the rest of us circled around him singing. 'The worms crawl in, the worms crawl out. They eat your guts and they spit them out.'

'It's *much* too noisy in here!' Mrs Horvath stood in our doorway with her hands on her hips. She is in charge of us during lunch. She's called a 'lunch teacher' but really she's more like a policewoman, patrolling the halls and sticking her head in and out of classrooms. We shut up in a hurry and scrambled back to our desks.

'What is that?' she asked, spying the apple on the floor.

Nobody answered.

'To whom does this apple belong?'

We all looked at Linda.

'Well?' Mrs Horvath said.

'It's mine,' Linda told her in a very weak voice.

'Food does not belong on the floor!' Mrs Horvath shouted.

'I know,' Linda said.

'Then why is it there?' Linda didn't say anything.

'Do you want me to report you to Mr Nichols?'

'No.'

'Then pick up that apple this instant!'

Linda hurried to the front of the room, picked up the apple, and dumped it into the trash basket.

'That's better,' Mrs Horvath said. 'Now, get into your jackets and go outside.'

uestions

1   Are the scenes described in this short story typical of what happens at lunchtime in any school? What do you think?

2. Explain why the author chose "Blubber" as the title of the story.

3   Imagine that you are Linda Fischer. Describe the incident in the classroom from your point of view. Mention in particular your feelings.

4. From the evidence of the story what type of person do you imagine Wendy to be? Explain your answer.

5. How do you think Mrs Horvath handled the incident with the apple? Give reasons for your opinion.

➤ The Confessional

SEÁN O'FAOLÁIN

In the wide nave the wintry evening light was faint as gloom and in the shadows of the aisle it was like early night. There was no sound in the chapel but the wind blowing up from the river valley, or an occasional tiny noise when a brass socket creaked under the great heat of a dying flame. To the three small boys crouched together on a bench in the farther aisle, holding each other's hands, listening timidly to the crying wind, staring wide-eyed at the candles, it seemed odd that in such a storm the bright flames never moved.

Suddenly the eldest of the three, a redheaded little ruffian, whispered loudly; but the other two, staring at the distant face of the statue, silenced him with a great hiss like a breaking wave. In another moment the lad in the centre, crouching down in fear and gripping the hand on each side of him, whispered so quietly that they barely heard, 'She's moving.'

For a second or two they did not even breathe. Then all three expelled a deep sigh of disappointment.

It was Monday afternoon, and every Monday, as they had each heard tell over and over again in their homes, Father Hanafin spoke with the Blessed Virgin in the grotto. Some said she came late at night; some said in the early morning before the chapel was opened; some said it was at the time when the sun goes down; but until now nobody had dared to watch. To be sure, Father Hanafin was not in the chapel now, but for all that the three little spies had come filled with high hope. The eldest spoke their bitter disappointment aloud.

'It's all my eye,' he said angrily. The other two felt that what he said was true, but they pretended to be deeply shocked.

'That's an awful thing you said, Foxer,' whispered the boy in the middle.

'Go away, you Philpot!' said Foxer.

'Gor! I think it's a cause for confession, Foxer!' whispered Philpot again.

'It's a mortal sin, Foxer!' said the third, leaning over to say it.

'Don't you try to cod me, Cooney, or I'll burst yer jaw!' cried Foxer angrily.

Philpot hushed them sternly and swiftly, but the spell was broken. They all leaned back in the bench.

Beside them was Father Hanafin's confession box, its worn purple curtain partly drawn back, his worn purple stole hanging on a crook on the wall inside, and as Foxer gazed into the box with curiosity the Adversary tempted him in his heart.

'Come on, Cooney!' he invited at last, 'Come on, and I'll hear yer confession.'

'Gor! Come on,' said Cooney, rising.

'That's a sin,' said Philpot, though secretly eager to sit in the priest's chair.

'You're an awful ould Aunt Mary!' jeered Foxer, whereupon all Philpot's scruples vanished and the three scrambled for the confessor's seat. But Foxer was there before either of them, and at once he swished the curtains together as he had seen Father Hanafin do, and put the long stole about his neck. It was so nice in there in the dark that he forgot his two penitents waiting beyond the closed grilles on either side, and he was putting imaginary snuff into his nostrils and flicking imaginary specks of snuff from his chest when

Cooney's angry face appeared between the curtains.

'Are yeh going to hear me confession, Foxer, or are yeh not?' he cried in a rage, eager for his turn to be priest.

'Go back, my child,' said Foxer crossly, and he swished the curtains together again. Then, as if in spite, he leaned over to the opposite grille and slowly and solemnly he drew the slide and peered into the frightened eyes of Philpot.

'Tell me how long since your last confession, my child,' he said gravely.

'Twenty years,' whispered Philpot in awe.

'What have you done since then?' intoned Foxer sadly.

'I stole sweets, Father. And I forgot my prayers. And I cursed, Father.'

'You cursed!' thundered Foxer. 'What curse did you say?'

'I said that our master was an ould sod, Father,' murmured Philpot timidly.

'So he is, my child. Is there anything else?'

'No, Father.'

'For your penance say two hundred and forty-nine Rosaries, and four hundred and seventy Our Fathers, and three hundred and thirty-two Hail Marys. And now be a good, obedient boy. And pray for me, won't you? Gawd bless you, my child.'

And with that Foxer drew the slide slowly before the small astonished face.

As he turned to the other side his hand fell on a little box it was Father Hanafin's consolation during the long hours spent in that stuffy confessional listening to the sins and sorrows of his parishioners.  Foxer's awkward fingers lifted the cover and the sweet scent rose powerfully through the darkness as he coaxed the loose snuff down from the cover. Then drawing the slide on Cooney, he gravely inhaled a pinch and leaned his ear to the cool iron of the grille.

Outside a footstep sounded on the marble floor, and peering out Foxer saw the priest walk slowly up the farther aisle, turn and walk slowly down again, his breviary held high to the slanting radiance of the Virgin's altar.

'It's Father Hanafin,' whispered Foxer to Cooney; and to Philpot, 'Keep quiet or we're all ruined.'

Up and down the solemn footsteps went, and high above their heads in the windows of the clerestory and along the lath and plaster of the roof the wind moaned and fingered the loose slates and now and again they heard the priest murmur aloud the deep open vowels of his prayer, *Gaudeamus Domine,* or *Domine, Domine meo,* in a long breathing sigh.

'He's talking to the Virgin,' breathed Cooney to Foxer.

'He's talking to the Virgin,' breathed Foxer in turn to Philpot.

'Amen,' sighed the priest, and went on his knees before the candles that shone steadily and were reflected brilliantly in the burnished brass.

The three spies had begun to peep from their hiding place when the snuff fell on Foxer's lap and the grains began to titillate his nose. In agony he held his mouth for a full minute and then burst into a furious sneeze. In astonishment the priest gazed about him and once again Foxer held his breath and once again he sneezed. At the third sneeze the priest gazed straight at the box.

'Come out!' he said in a loud voice. 'Come out of that box'

And as the three guilty forms crept from the three portals he commanded again, 'Come here!'

Awkwardly they stumbled forward through the seats, trying to hide behind one another, pushing and upbraiding one another until they stood before him.

'What were you doing in there?' he asked Foxer.

'I was hearing their confession, Father,' trembled Foxer, and half raised his arm as if to ward off a blow.

For a moment the priest glared at him and then he asked, 'And what penance did you give?'

'I -- I gave three hundred and thirty-two Hail Marys, Father, and I think it was four hundred Our Fathers, Father, and two hundred and forty-nine Rosaries, Father.'

'Well!' pronounced the priest in a solemn voice. 'Go home and let each one of ye say that penance three times over before nine o'clock tomorrow morning.'

Stumbling over one another's heels the three crept down the dark aisle and crushed out through the green baize door and into the falling night that was torn by the storm. The street lamps were lit and under one of these they halted and looked at each other, angry and crestfallen.

'Nine hundred and ninety Hail Marys!' wailed Philpot, and Cooney squared up to Foxer with clenched fists.

'Yerrah!' said Foxer. 'It's all a cod!'

And he raced suddenly away to his supper, followed by the shouts and feet of the other two.

from *Stories of Seán O Faoláin*

uestions

1 Describe the atmosphere in the church at the start of this story.
2 What does the writer mean by the line 'the Adversary tempted him in his heart'?
3 From the evidence of this story, what type of boy do you imagine Foxer to be? Have you ever met anybody like him? Describe that person.
4 Write a character sketch of Fr. Hanafin as he appears in this story.
5 How would you describe the boys attitude to religion? Support your answer by reference to the story.
6 This story could easily be written in the form of a short play. What elements of the story make this possible?
7 Frightened: brave: mischievous:
   All three adjectives can be used to describe the boys. Explain why this is true.

▶ The Hitch-hiker

ROALD DAHL

I had a new car. It was an exciting toy, a big B.M.W. 3•3 Li, which means 3•3 litre, long wheelbase, fuel injection. I had a top speed of 129 m.p.h. and terrific acceleration. The body was pale blue. The seats inside were darker blue and they were made of leather, genuine soft leather of the finest quality. The windows were electrically operated and so was the sun-roof. The radio aerial popped up when I switched on the radio, and disappeared when I switched it off. The powerful engine growled and grunted impatiently at slow speeds, but at sixty miles an hour the growling stopped and the motor began to purr with pleasure.

I was driving up to London by myself. It was a lovely June day. They were haymaking in the fields and there were buttercups along both sides of the road. I was whispering along at seventy miles an hour, leaning back comfortably in my seat, with no more than a couple of fingers resting lightly on the wheel to keep her steady. Ahead of me I saw a man thumbing a lift. I touched the foot-brake and brought the car to a stop beside him. I always stopped for hitch-hikers. I knew just how it used to feel to be standing on the side of a country road watching the cars go by. I hated the drivers for pretending they didn't see me, especially the ones in big cars with three empty seats. The large expensive cars seldom stopped. It was always the smaller ones that offered you a lift, or the old rusty ones, or the ones that were already crammed full of children and the driver would say, 'I think we can squeeze in one more.'

The hitch-hiker poked his head through the open window and said, 'Going to London, guv'nor?'

'Yes,' I said, 'Jump in.'

He got in and I drove on.

He was a small ratty-faced man with grey teeth. His eyes were dark and quick and clever, like a rat's eyes, and his ears were slightly pointed at the top. He had a cloth cap on his head and he was wearing a greyish-coloured jacket with enormous pockets. The grey jacket, together with the quick eyes and the pointed ears, made him look more than anything like some sort of a huge human rat.

'What part of London are you headed for?' I asked him.

'I'm goin' right through London and out the other side,' he said. 'I'm goin' to Epsom, for the races. It's Derby Day today.'

'So it is,' I said. 'I wish I were going with you. I love betting on horses.'

'I never bet on horses,' he said. 'I don't even watch 'em run. That's stupid silly business.'

'Then why do you go?' I asked.

He didn't seem to like that question. His little ratty face went absolutely blank and he sat there staring straight ahead at the road, saying nothing.

'I expect you help to work the betting machines or something like that,' I said.

'That's even sillier,' he answered. 'There's no fun working them lousy machines and selling tickets to mugs. Any fool could do that.'

There was a long silence. I decided not to question him any more. I remembered how irritated I used to get in my hitch-hiking days when drivers kept asking *me* questions. Where are you going? Why are you going there? What's your job? Are you married? Do you have a girl-friend? What's her name? How old are you? And so on and so forth. I used to hate it.

'I'm sorry,' I said. 'It's none of my business what you do. The trouble is, I'm a writer, and most writers are terrible nosy parkers.'

'You write books?' he asked.

'Yes.'

'Writin' books is okay,' he said. 'It's what I call a skilled trade. I'm in a skilled trade too. The folks I despise is them that spend all their lives doin' crummy old routine jobs with no skill in em' at all. You see what I mean?'

'Yes.'

'The secret of life,' he said, 'is to become very very good at somethin' that's very very 'ard to do.'

'Like you,' I said.

'Exactly. You and me both.'

'What makes you think that *I'm* any good at my job?' I asked. 'There's an awful lot of bad writers around.'

'You wouldn't be drivin' about in a car like this if you weren't no good at it,' he answered. 'It must've cost a tidy packet, this little job.'

'It wasn't cheap.'

'What can she do flat out?' he asked.

'One hundred and twenty-nine miles an hour,' I told him.

'I'll bet she won't do it.'

'I'll bet she will.'

'All car makers is liars,' he said.'You can buy any car you like and it'll never do what the makers say it will in the ads.'

'This one will.'

'Open 'er up then and prove it,' he said. 'Go on, guv'nor, open 'er right up and let's see what she'll do.'

There is a roundabout at Chalfont St Peter and immediately beyond it there's a long straight section of dual carriageway. We came out of the roundabout on to the carriageway and I pressed my foot down on the accelerator. The big car leaped forward as though she'd been stung. In ten seconds or so, we were doing ninety.

'Lovely!' he cried. 'Beautiful! Keep goin'!'

I had the accelerator jammed right down against the floor and I held it there.

'One hundred!' he shouted...'A hundred and five!...A hundred and ten!...A hundred and fifteen! Go on! Don't slack off!'

I was in the outside lane and we flashed past several cars as though they were standing still — a green Mini, a big cream-coloured Citroën, a white Land-Rover, a huge truck with a container on the back, an orange-coloured Volkswagen Minibus...

'A hundred and twenty!' my passenger shouted, jumping up and down. 'Go on! Go on! Get 'er up to one-two-nine!'

At that moment, I heard the scream of a police siren. It was so loud it seemed to be right inside the car, and then a policeman on a motor-cycle loomed up alongside us on the inside lane and went past us and raised a hand for us to stop.

'Oh, my sainted aunt!' I said. 'That's torn it!'

The policeman must have been doing about a hundred and thirty when he passed us, and he took plenty of time slowing down. Finally, he pulled into the side of the road and I pulled in behind him. 'I didn't know police motor-cycles could go as fast as that,' I said rather lamely.

'That one can,' my passenger said. 'It's the same make as yours. It's a B.M.W. R90S. Fastest bike on the road. That's what they're usin' nowadays.'

The policeman got off his motor-cycle and leaned the machine sideways on to its prop stand. Then he took off his gloves and placed them carefully on the seat. He was in no hurry now. He had us where he wanted us and he knew it.

'This is real trouble,' I said. 'I don't like it one bit.'

'Don't talk to 'im any more than is necessary, you understand,' my companion said. 'Just sit tight and keep mum.'

Like an executioner approaching his victim, the policeman came strolling slowly towards us. He was a big meaty man with a belly, and his blue breeches were skintight around his enormous thighs. His goggles were pulled up on the helmet, showing a smouldering red face with wide cheeks.

We sat there like guilty schoolboys, waiting for him to arrive.

'Watch out for this man,' my passenger whispered. "Ee looks mean as the devil.'

The policeman came round to my open window and placed one meaty hand on the sill. 'What's the hurry?' he said.

'No hurry, officer,' I answered.

'Perhaps there's a woman in the back having a baby and you're rushing her to hospital? Is that it?'

'No, officer.'

'Or perhaps you house is on fire and you're dashing home to rescue the family from upstairs?' His voice was dangerously soft and mocking.

'My house isn't on fire, officer.'

'In that case,' he said, 'you've got yourself into a nasty mess, haven't you? Do you know what the speed limit is in this country?'

'Seventy,' I said.

'And do you mind telling me exactly what speed you were doing just now?'

I shrugged and didn't say anything.

When he spoke next, he raised his voice so loud that I jumped. *One hundred and twenty miles per hour!* he barked. 'That's *fifty* miles an hour over the limit!'

He turned his head and spat out a big gob of spit. It landed on the wing of my car and started sliding down over my beautiful blue paint. Then he turned back again and stared hard at my passenger. 'And who are you?' he asked sharply.

'He's a hitch-hiker,' I said. 'I'm giving him a lift.'

''Ave I done somethin' wrong?' my passenger asked.

His voice was as soft and oily as haircream.

'That's more than likely,' the policeman answered.

'Anyway, you're a witness. I'll deal with you in a minute. Driving-licence,' he snapped, holding out his hand.

I gave him my driving-licence.

He unbuttoned the left-hand breast-pocket of his tunic and brought out the dreaded books of tickets. Carefully, he copied the name and address from my licence. Then he gave it back to me. He strolled round to the front of the car and read the number from the number-plate and wrote that down as well. He filled in the date, the time and the details of my offence. Then he tore out the top copy of the ticket. But before handing it to me, he checked that all the information had come through clearly on his own carbon copy. Finally, he replaced the book in his tunic pocket and fastened the button.

'Now you,' he said to my passenger, and he walked around to the other side of the car. From the other breast-pocket he produced a small black notebook.

'Name?' he snapped.

'Michael Fish,' my passenger said.

'Address?'

'Fourteen, Windsor Lane, Luton.'

'Show me something to prove this is your real name and address,' the policeman said.

My passenger fished in his pockets and came out with a driving-licence of his own. The policeman checked the name and address and handed it back to him.

'What's your job?' he asked sharply.

'I'm an 'od carrier.'

'A *what?*'

'An 'od carrier.'

'Spell it.'

'H-O-D C-A-...'

'That'll do. And what's a hod carrier, may I ask?'

'An 'od carrier, officer, is a person 'oo carries the cement up the ladder to the bricklayer. And the 'od is what 'ee carries it in. It's got a long 'andle, and on the top you've got two bits of wood set at an angle...'

'All right, all right. Who's your employer?'

'Don't 'ave one. I'm unemployed.'

The policeman wrote all this down in the black notebook. Then he returned the book to its pocket and did up the button.

'When I get back to the station I'm going to do a little checking up on you,' he said to my passenger.

'Me? What've I done wrong?' the rat-faced man asked.

'I don't like your face, that's all,' the policeman said. 'And we just might have a picture of it somewhere in our files.' He strolled round the car and returned to my window.

'I suppose you know you're in serious trouble,' he said to me.

'Yes, officer.'

'You won't be driving this fancy car of yours again for a very long time, not after we've finished with you. You won't be driving *any* car again come to that for several years. And a good thing, too. I hope they lock you up for a spell into the bargain.'

'You mean prison?' I asked, alarmed.

'Absolutely,' he said, smacking his lips. 'In the clink. Behind the bars. Along with all the other criminals who break the law. *And* a hefty fine into the bargain. Nobody will be more pleased about that than me. I'll see you in court, both of you. You'll be getting a summons to appear.'

He turned away and walked over to his motor-cycle.

He flipped the prop stand back into position with his foot and swung his leg over the saddle. Then he kicked the starter and roared off up the road out of sight.

'Phew!' I gasped. 'That's done it.'

'We was caught,' my passenger said. 'We was caught good and proper.'

'I was caught, you mean.'

'That's right,' he said. 'What you goin' to do now, guv'nor?'

'I'm going straight up to London to talk to my solicitor,' I said. I started the car and drove on.

'You mustn't believe what 'ee said to you about goin' to prison,' my passenger said. 'They don't put nobody in the clink just for speedin'.'

'Are you sure of that?' I asked.

'I'm positive,' he answered. 'They can take your licence away and they can give you a whoppin' big fine, but that'll be the end of it.'

I felt tremendously relieved.

'By the way,' I said, 'why did you lie to him?'

'Who, me?' he said. 'What makes you think I lied?'

'You told him you were an unemployed hod carrier. But you told *me* you were in a highly-skilled trade.'

'So I am,' he said. 'But it don't pay to tell everythin' to a copper.'

'So what *do* you do?' I asked him.

'Ah,' he said slyly. 'That'd be tellin', wouldn't it?'

'Is it something you're ashamed of?'

'Ashamed?' he cried. 'Me, ashamed of my job? I'm about as proud of it as anybody could be in the entire world!'

'Then why won't you tell me?'

'You writers really is nosey parkers, aren't you?' he said. 'And you ain't goin' to be 'appy, I don't think, until you've found out exactly what the answer is?'

'I don't really care one way or the other,' I told him, lying.

He gave me a crafty little ratty look out of the sides of his eyes. 'I think you do care,' he said. 'I can see it in your face that you think I'm in some kind of a very peculiar trade and you're just achin' to know what it is.'

I didn't like the way he read my thoughts. I kept quiet and stared at the road ahead.

'You'd be right, too,' he went on. 'I *am* in a very peculiar trade. I'm in the queerest peculiar trade of 'em all.'

I waited for him to go on.

'That's why I 'as to be extra careful 'oo I'm talkin' to, you see. 'Ow am I to know, for instance, you're not another copper in plain clothes?'

'Do I look like a copper?'

'No,' he said. 'You don't. And you ain't. Any fool could tell that.'

He took from his pocket a tin of tobacco and a packet of cigarette papers and started to roll a cigarette. I was watching him out of the corner of one eye, and the speed with which he performed this rather difficult operation was incredible. The cigarette was rolled and ready in about five seconds. He ran his tongue along the edge of the paper, stuck it down and popped the cigarette between his lips. Then, as if from nowhere, a lighter appeared in his hand. The lighter flamed. The cigarette was lit. The lighter disappeared. It was altogether a remarkable performance.

'I've never seen anyone roll a cigarette as fast as that,' I said.

'Ah,' he said, taking a deep suck of smoke. 'So you noticed.'

'Of course I noticed. It was quite fantastic.'

He sat back and smiled. It pleased him very much that I had noticed how quickly he could roll a cigarette. 'You want to know what makes me able to do it?' he asked.

'Go on then.'

'It's because I've got fantastic fingers. These fingers of mine,' he said, holding up both hands high in front of him, 'are quicker and cleverer than the fingers of the best piano player in the world!'

'Are you a piano player?'

'Don't be daft,' he said. 'Do I look like a piano player?'

I glanced at his fingers. They were so beautifully shaped, so slim and long and elegant, they didn't seem to belong to the rest of him at all. They looked more like the fingers of a brain surgeon or a watchmaker.

'My job,' he went on, 'is a hundred times more difficult than playin' the piano. Any twerp can learn to do that. There's titchy little kids learnin' to play the piano in almost any 'ouse you go into these days. That's right, ain't it?'

'More or less,' I said.

'Of course it's right. But there's not one person in ten million can learn to do what I do. Not one in ten million! 'Ow about that?'

'Amazing,' I said.

'You're darn right it's amazin',' he said.

'I think I know what you do,' I said. 'You do conjuring tricks. You're a conjurer.'

'Me?' he snorted. 'A conjurer? Can you picture me goin' round crummy kids' parties makin' rabbits come out of top 'ats?'

'Then you're a card player. You get people into card games and deal yourself marvellous hands.'

'Me! A rotten card-sharper!' he cried. 'That's a miserable racket if ever there was one.'

'All right. I give up.'

I was taking the car along slowly now, at no more than forty miles an hour, to make quite sure I wasn't stopped again. We had come on to the main London–Oxford road and were running down the hill towards Denham.

Suddenly, my passenger was holding up a black leather belt in his hand. 'Ever seen this before?' he asked. The belt had a brass buckle of unusual design.

'Hey!' I said. 'That's mine, isn't it? It *is* mine! Where did you get it?'

He grinned and waved the belt gently from side to side. 'Where d'you think I got it?' he said. 'Off the top of your trousers, of course.'

I reached down and felt for my belt. It was gone.

'You mean you took it off me while we've been driving along?' I asked, flabbergasted.

He nodded, watching me all the time with those little black ratty eyes.

'That's impossible,' I said. 'You'd have to undo the buckle and slide the whole thing out through the loops all the way round. I'd have seen you doing it. And even if I hadn't seen you, I'd have felt it.'

'Ah, but you didn't, did you?' he said, triumphant. He dropped the belt on his lap, and now all at once there was a brown shoelace dangling from his fingers. 'And what about his, then?' he exclaimed, waving the shoelace.

'What about it?' I said.

'Anyone round 'ere missin' a shoelace?' he asked. grinning.

I glanced down at my shoes. The lace of one of them was missing. 'Good grief!' I said. 'How did you do that? I never saw you bending down.'

'You never saw nothin',' he said proudly. 'You never even saw me move an inch. And you know why?'

'Yes,' I said. 'Because you've got fantastic fingers.'

'Exactly right!' he cried. 'You catch on pretty quick, don't you?' He sat back and sucked away at his home-made cigarette, blowing the smoke out in a thin stream against the windshield. He knew he had impressed me greatly with those two tricks, and this made him very happy. 'I don't want to be late,' he said. 'What time is it?'

'There's a clock in front of you,' I told him.

'I don't trust car clocks,' he said. 'What does your watch say?'

I hitched up my sleeve to look at the watch on my wrist. It wasn't there. I looked at the man. He looked back at me, grinning.

'You've taken that, too,' I said.

He held out his hand and there was my watch lying in his palm. 'Nice bit of stuff, this,' he said. 'Superior quality. Eighteen-carat gold. Easy to flog, too. It's never any trouble gettin' rid of quality goods.'

'I'd like it back, if you don't mind.' I said rather huffily.

He placed the watch carefully on the leather tray in front of him. 'I wouldn't nick anything from you, guv'nor,' he said. 'You're my pal. You're giving me a lift.'

'I'm glad to hear it,' I said.

'All I'm doin' is answerin' your questions,' he went on. 'You asked me what I did for a livin' and I'm showin' you.'

'What else have you got of mine?'

He smiled again, and now he started to take from the pocket of his jacket one thing after another that belonged to me — my driving-licence, a key-ring with four keys on it, some pound notes, a few coins, a letter from my publishers, my diary, a stubby old pencil, a cigarette-lighter, and last of all, a beautiful old sapphire ring with pearls around it belonging to my wife. I was taking the ring up to the jeweller in London because one of the pearls was missing.

'Now *there's* another lovely piece of goods,' he said, turning the ring over in his fingers. 'That's eighteenth century, if I'm not mistaken, from the reign of King George the Third.'

'You're right,' I said, impressed. 'You're absolutely right.'

He put the ring on the leather tray with the other items.

'So you're a pickpocket,' I said.

'I don't like that word,' he answered. 'It's a coarse and vulgar word. Pickpockets is coarse and vulgar people who only do easy little amateur jobs. They lift money from blind old ladies.'

'What do you call yourself, then?'

'Me? I'm a fingersmith. I'm a professional fingersmith.' He spoke the words solemnly and proudly, as though he were telling me he was the President of the Royal College of Surgeons or the Archbishop of Canterbury.

'I've never heard that word before,' I said. 'Did you invent it?'

'Of course I didn't invent it,' he replied. 'It's the name given to them who's risen to the very top of the profession. You've 'eard of a goldsmith and a silversmith, for instance. They're experts with gold and silver. I'm an expert with my fingers, so I'm a fingersmith.'

'It must be an interesting job.'

'It's a marvellous job,' he answered. 'It's lovely.'

'And that's why you go to the races?'

'Race meetings is easy meat,' he said. 'You just stand around after the race, watchin' for the lucky ones to queue up and draw their money. And when you see someone collectin' a big bundle of notes, you simply follows after 'im and 'elps yourself. But don't get me wrong, guv'nor. I never takes nothin' from a loser. Nor from poor people neither. I only go after them as can afford it, the winners and the rich.'

'That's very thoughtful of you,' I said. 'How often do you get caught?'

'Caught?' he cried, disgusted. '*Me* get caught! It's only pickpockets get caught. Fingersmiths never. Listen, I could take the false teeth out of your mouth if I wanted to and you wouldn't even catch me!'

'I don't have false teeth,' I said.

'I know you don't,' he answered. 'Otherwise I'd 'ave 'ad 'em out long ago!'

I believed him. Those long slim fingers of his seemed able to do anything.

We drove on for a while without talking.

'That policeman's going to check up on you pretty thoroughly,' I said. 'Doesn't that worry you a bit?'

'Nobody's checkin' up on me,' he said.

'Of course they are. He's got your name and address written down most carefully in his black book.'

The man gave me another of his sly, ratty little smiles. 'Ah,' he said. 'So 'ee 'as. But I'll bet 'ee ain't got it all written down in 'is memory as well. I've never known a copper yet with a decent memory. Some of 'em can't even remember their own names.'

'What's memory got to do with it?' I asked. 'It's written down in his book, isn't it?'

'Yes, guv'nor, it is. But the trouble is, 'ee's lost the book. 'Ee's lost both books, the one with my name in it *and* the one with yours.'

In the long delicate fingers of his right hand, the man was holding up in triumph the two books he had taken from the policeman's pockets. 'Easiest job I ever done,' he announced proudly.

I nearly swerved the car into a milk-truck, I was so excited.

'That copper's got nothin' on either of us now,' he said.

'You're a genius!' I cried.

"Ee's got no names, no addresses, no car number, no nothin',' he said.

'You're brilliant!'

'I think you'd better pull in off this main road as soon as possible,' he said. 'Then we'd better build a little bonfire and burn these books.'

'You're a fantastic fellow,' I exclaimed.

'Thank you, guv'nor,' he said. 'It's always nice to be appreciated.'

Roald Dahl from *The Wonderful Story of Henry Sugar*

Questions

1 Why do you think the author describes the car in such detail?
2 In what ways are the driver and the hitch-hiker different from one another?
3 'I've never seen anybody roll a cigarette as fast as that'. This sentence is meant to prepare us for what follows. Explain in what way this is true.
4 Write a character sketch of the hitch-hiker as he appears in the story.
5 Suggest another title for this short story by Roald Dahl and give reasons for your choice.
6 The story contains a lot of dialogue. What does the use of dialogue contribute to the overall effect of this short story?
7 The author uses a number of slang words in the story. Select some examples, explain what they mean and what the use of this type of language contributes to the story.

➤ Janey Mary

JAMES PLUNKETT

When Janey Mary turned the corner into Nicholas Street that morning, she leaned wearily against a shop-front to rest. Her small head was bowed and the hair which was so nondescript and unclean covered her face. Her small hands gripped one another for warmth across the faded bodice of her frock. Around the corner lay Canning Cottages with their tiny, frost-gleaming gardens, and gates that were noisy and freezing to touch. She had tried each of them in turn. Her timid knock was well known to the people who lived in Canning Cottages. That morning some of them said: 'It's that little 'Carthy one, never mind opening. Twice in the last week she's been around, it's too much of a good thing.' Those who did answer her had been dour. They poked cross and harassed faces around half-open doors. Tell her mammy, they said, it's at school she should have her, and not out worrying poor people the likes of them. They had the mouths of their own to feed and the bellies of their own to fill and God knows that took doing.

The school was in Nicholas Street and children with satchels were already passing. Occasionally Janey Mary could see a few paper books peeping from an open flap, and beside them a child's lunch and a bottle of milk. In the schoolroom was a scrawled and incomprehensible blackboard and rows of staring faces which sniggered when Janey Mary was stupid in her answers.

Sometimes Father Benedict would visit the school. He asked questions in Catechism and gave the children sweets. He was a huge man who had more intuition than intellect, more genuine affection for children than for learning. One day he found Janey Mary sitting by herself in the back desk. She felt him, giant-like above her, bending over her. Some wrapped sweets were put on her desk.

'And what's your name, little girl?'

'Janey Mary 'Carthy, Father.'

'I'm Father Benedict of the Augustinians. Where do you live?' Father Benedict had pushed his way and shoved his way until he was sitting in the desk beside her. Quite suddenly Janey Mary had felt safe and warm. She said easily, 'I lives in Canning Cottages.'

He talked to her while the teacher continued self-consciously with her lesson.

'So, your daddy works in the meat factory?'

'No, Father, my daddy's dead.'

Father Benedict nodded and patted her shoulder. 'You and I must be better friends, Janey,' he said. 'We must tell your mammy to send you to school more often.'

'Yes, Father.'

'Because we must see more of one another, mustn't we?'

'Yes, Father.'

'Would you always come?'

'I'd like to come, Father.'

Father Benedict had talked with her for some time like that, the pair of them crushed clumsily in the desk and their heads close together. When he was leaving he gave her more sweets. Later the teacher took them from her as a punishment and gave them out again as little prizes for neatness.

She thought of Father Benedict until an old beggar who was passing said to her: 'Are you whingin', child? Is there anything up with you?'

She lifted her head and looked stupidly at him, her mouth open and her eyes quite dry. He was a humpbacked man with broken boots and a bulbous nose. The street about him was a moving forest of feet; the stolid tread of workmen and the pious shuffle of middle-aged women on their way from Mass.

'You look a bit shook, kid,' he said. 'Are you after taking a turn?'

'No, mister,' she said, wondering. 'I'm only going for to look for bread at St. Nicholas's. My mammy told me.'

'Your mammy left it a bit late. They'll be going in for to pray.' As though awakened by his words, the bell of the Augustinian Friary rang three times. It rang out with long, resounding strokes across the quivering street, and people paused to uncover their heads and to bless themselves.

Janey Mary looked up quickly. The steeple of the church rose clear and gleaming above the tall houses, and the golden slimness of its cross raced swiftly against the blue and gold of the sky.

Her mother had said: 'Look till you find, my lady, and you won't lose your labour. This is the day of the Blessed Bread and if you get it nowhere else they'll be giving it out at St. Nicholas's.'

She turned suddenly and ran quickly up the length of the street. But when she reached the priory the doors were closed and the waiting queue had broken into small knots. She stopped uncertainly and stared for some time.

The priests, the people said, had gone in to pray. they would be back in an hour.

She was glad to turn homewards. She was tired and her bare feet moved reluctantly on the ice-cold pavement. Johnny might have been given some bread on his round with the sticks, or her mother might have had some hidden away. Her mother sometimes did that so that Janey Mary would try very hard to get some.

Picking her way amongst the debris-littered wasteland upon which houses had once stood, she watched her shadow bobbing and growing with the uneven rippling of the ground. The light of the wintry sun rested wanly on everything and the sky was dizzily blue and fluffed a little with white cloud. There were rust-eaten tin-cans lying neglected on the waste, and fragments of coloured delf which she could have gathered to play chaneys had she had the time. The children often went there to play shop; they marked out their pitches with a file of pebbles in the form of an open square. When Janey Mary stood in one of the squares for a moment she was no longer Janey Mary. The waste-land became a busy street and the tracery of pebbles glittering stores. Her face would grow grave. It was that serene gravity of a child at play. But when she stepped out of the magic square she was again Janey Mary, a Janey Mary who was cold and hungry and whose mother was waiting impatiently for bread that had not been found.

'There was none,' she said, looking up at her mother's face. 'Nobody would give it and the man said the priests wouldn't be back for an hour.' She looked around hopefully as she spoke, but there were only a few crumbs on the table. They littered its grease-fouled and flower-patterned covering. An enamel jug stood in the centre and about it the slopped ugliness of used cups. Now that she was home she realised how endless the morning's trudging had been. She realised how every door had been closed against her. Her mother's voice rose.

'Then you can do without. Are you after looking at all, you little trollop? Two hours to go the length of the street and around to the holy priests, and us all in a wakeness with the hunger. And Johnny going out with the sticks and him famished but for the little bit I had left away. Are you after looking at all?'

The enamel of the jug was broken in three places. The breaks were spidery, like the blobs of ink which used to fall so dishearteningly on her copy-books. Down the side of each cup clung the yellow residue of dribbled tea. The whole table shifted suddenly and went back again, and her mother's voice seemed far away. Janey Mary wanted to sit down.

'Gallivanting,' her mother said, 'off gallivanting with your pals. I'll gallivant you. But you can go back again. There's nothing in the house. Back with you to the priests' house and wait like any Christian for what's going. And take the bag with you. You don't do a hand's turn till you do that.'

Janey Mary stood with her hands clasped in front of her and looked up at her mother. The thought of going back again filled her with misery.

'I asked,' she said. 'I asked everywhere.'

'Then you can ask again,' said her mother. 'You can ask till you find,' and swung away. Janey Mary went wearily to the corner to fetch the bag. The kitchen trembled and became dark when she bent to pick it up. As she went out of the door her mother said:

'Put a bit of hurry on yourself and don't be slingeing. It's certain you'll never die with the beating of your heart. The world and its wife would get something and mine'd be left.'

Once more she went out in the ancient crookedness of streets, picking her way amidst the trundling of wheels and the countless feet. Tiny and lost beneath the steepness of houses, she went slowly, her bare feet dragging and dirty. At this hour the shops in Nicholas Street were crowded with women who haggled over halfpennies. White-coated assistants leaned quickly over marble-topped counters with heads cocked to one side and pencils raised in readiness, or dashed from counters to shelves and back again, banging things on the scales and then licking pencil stubs while they frowned over figures. Sometimes Janey Mary used to stand and watch them, but now she went by without interest. When a tram went grinding past her, her lips trembled, and though the rails after it and before it gleamed in the sunlight, it was a pale cold gleaming. There was no friendly heat in the sunlight. There was nothing friendly. There were only trundling trams and the tramp of feet, and once again the slim cross on the spire of St. Nicholas's.

On the Feast of the Blessed Bread it was the custom of the priests to erect a wooden counter on the high steps before the door of the priory. Here two of the brothers stood to watch the forming of the queue. Janey Mary looked hard through the veil which blurred occasionally in front of her eyes, but could catch no sign of Father Benedict. No bread had yet appeared though the queue was growing. She took her place and kept close to the wall. In near the wall she found it easier to hold her position. It was very cold at first, but after a while more people came and the air grew warmer. They came, as she had known they would, with baskets and shawls with torn shopping bags and ragged coats, and gathered thickly about her. There were men there too, old pensioners and men who had not worked for years.

'There won't be much going,' they said. 'There was a shocking crowd here this morning.'

'Take your bloody hour,' they said. 'Who d'you think you're pushing?'

'Aisy, aisy, mind the chisler.'

They talked like that for a long time. At first they argued furiously with one another. But later they became dour with impatience. They shuffled uncomfortably. They spat frequently and heaved long sighs.

After a while it became frightening to be in there so close to the wall, to be so small that everyone towered over you. Janey Mary felt weak and wanted to get out. When she glanced sideways or ahead of her she could see nothing but tightly packed bodies, and when she looked down there were feet, but no ground. She tried to look upwards, but could not. An hour passed before Father Benedict appeared on the steps.

'Father Benedict, God bless him,' they said. 'It'll be coming soon when he's there.'

Janey Mary was lifted clear off the ground by the movement of the crowd and lost her place. Now she was behind a stooping-backed man with a threadbare coat and heavily nailed boots. His collar was flaked and greasy with dandruff and his coat was foul smelling, but it was the boots which held Janey Mary's attention. They clattered unsteadily on the pavement very close to her bare feet. There were diamond-shaped nails in double rings about the heels of them. She bent to keep her eyes fixed on the boots and wriggled to avoid them. Her attention became fixed on them. To a man near her she said, 'I want to get out, mister, let me get out,' but even if he heard her he could not have helped her now. She tried to attract attention, but they had forgotten her. They kept telling one another over and over again what each of them already knew.

'It's coming,' they said, pressing forward, 'it's coming.' And after a while the murmuring changed and the queue surged.

'Look,' they shouted, 'it's here.'

Janey Mary was lifted once more. Once more her feet were clear of the ground and her breathing stifled by the pressure of those around her. She was in danger now and clawed whimpering at the dandruff-flaked collar. Through the whirl of arms and shoulders she had a view of Father Benedict, his broad shoulders tall and firm above the press of bodies. She tried to call out to him.

'The chisler,' someone said, noticing. 'For God's sake quit pushing. Look at the chisler.' A man threw out his hand to grip her, but a movement of the crowd twisted him suddenly aside. She saw his hand grabbing futilely to her left. As the crowd parted she began to slip.

'Father Benedict,' she called faintly, 'Father Benedict.' Then the man in front stumbled and the nailed boots crushed heavily on her feet.

When her eyes opened again she was on the sofa in the visitors' parlour. Father Benedict and one of the lay brothers were bending over her. Someone had put a rug about her. An electric fire glowed warmly against the opposite wall, and over it hung a gold-framed picture of the Sacred Heart. Her feet felt numb and heavy and the picture swam before her eyes. But it was warm in the parlour and the morning's searching was over. Then she remembered the bread and her mother's words. She moved suddenly, but when she tried to speak her ears were filled with noise. The lay brother had turned to Father Benedict.

'You were very quick,' he was saying. 'Is she badly hurt?'

Father Benedict, answering him, said in a strange voice:

'Only her feet...You can see the print of the nails...'

James Plunkett

Questions

1   What evidence is there in the story to show that the teacher was not very kind to Janey Mary?
2   From the evidence of the story what type of woman do you think Janey Mary's mother was? Support your answer by reference to the story.
3   Janey Mary liked to play shop on the wasteland. What does this tell you about her character?
4   As the story progresses the tension builds to a climax. How does the author achieve this effect?
5   How would you describe the mood or atmosphere in this story? Explain your answer.
6   This story contains a number of religious images. Select some examples and say what they contribute to the story.
7   Imagine that you are Father Benedict. Write an account of what happened on the Feast of the Blessed Bread from your point of view.

➤ Trio

JENNIFER JOHNSTON

In spite of the brilliant, sliding sun the evening was cold. Frank pushed his hands deep down into his pockets and stamped his feet uselessly.

'What a wind!'

Dust and an empty cigarette-box skeltered past their feet, down the hill past the waiting gateways and the neat hedges.

'West. It's from the west. That means rain. More rain. God, I'll be glad when this winter's over.'

Murphy pulled on his cigarette and let the smoke trickle slowly out through his nose. He was wearing a knitted hat pulled well down over his ears.

Frank shuffled his feet on the pavement again.

'I get chilblains,' he complained. 'Every bloody winter. There's nothing you can do about it. There was one year I didn't, that was the time I was working in London. It's the damp. So they say. Drive you crazy sometimes, so they would. Just that one year I didn't get them.'

Murphy sighed. Talkers. He was always lumbered with a talker. Voices always nagging away, nudging their way into his head, never letting him be at peace with his own thoughts. Silence was good. Golden, his mother used to say. He turned and squinted his eyes towards the setting sun. Golden, but you couldn't see with it dazzling in your eyes, even when you turned your head away again you couldn't focus for a moment or two. He walked back up the street towards the main road. With a bit of luck the sun would be behind the hill in about ten minutes.

'Did you ever suffer with chilblains?' asked Frank behind him.

'No.' 'You wouldn't know then what it's like at all.'

'No.'

They stood at the corner for a few moments, watching the cars go by. Behind them, below where they had been standing a man sat, reading a book, in a parked car. Murphy dropped the butt of his cigarette on the pavement on the pavement and then put his foot on it.

'What's the time?'

Murphy looked at his watch.

'Ten to.'

'He's late.'

They stared across the valley at the distant hills, the glitter.

'It'd be a great evening if it wasn't so cold. Maybe he'll not come.'

They turned and strolled back down the road again.

'He'll come all right.'

Patrick opened the door of his car and threw his briefcase over onto the back seat. Late.

He got into the car and slammed the door. Meticulously he placed his thin white hands on the steering wheel and stared at them. What does it matter anyway? Late or early. Nobody else worries. No one gets agitated. We all have our own obsessions. I like to treat time with care. He started the engine and sat listening to the comfortable sound of it. Like a cat by the fire. What precisely do I consider myself to be late for? The small preoccupations of domestic life. The kiss on the cheek. The careful arrangement of glasses on a tray. Clink, clink across the hall, taking care not to slip on the Persian carpet. Last shafts of sun and then pull the curtains, keep our privacy to ourselves. No dreams. No time for dreams. The stir and tumult of defeated dreams... who could have said that? From those years when I read books and nervously brooded on the meanings of things. I must tidy things up and have a break. I'm tired. He laughed and moved the car slowly forward across the yard. A break indeed. What happens I wonder when you, for a moment, realise the emptiness of the future, oh and God the past. The dreamlessness even of the past. Forget it. Impeccable safety.

'Good evening, sir.'

George, the security man, opened the gate into the street. Patrick smiled and nodded. 'You're late tonight, sir. It's ten to.'

'Telephones should never have been invented.'

'Goodnight.'

'Goodnight, George. See you in the morning.'

'Of course he'll come.'

'But if he doesn't? What do we do?'

'We come back tomorrow.'

Murphy's voice was exasperated.

The wind was banging at their backs, pushing them firmly down the hill.

'I suppose we would.' Frank sighed. 'My sister's just been took into the hospital. Just, there a few minutes before I came out. Her first. Ay. I know she'll be expecting me up to see her tomorrow.'

The way of the world, thought Murphy, one goes, another comes. Apart from his own somewhat amazed arrival into the world, he has no close, touching experiences of either birth or death. It didn't do to look at he whole thing in a broad, emotional way. Achievement was what mattered.

'That is, if he comes...'

Murphy's cap had worked its way up onto the top of his head. He pulled it firmly, warmly down over his ears again.

The gate closed behind him. The traffic was edging slowly along between the high warehouses. Time, as usual, being wasted, maltreated. Then suppose, just suppose that I treated time as if it belonged to me. I am no longer time's servant. What then? It becomes at once a precious commodity. The only one worth having. Will I turn on the radio and listen to the news? Drown the sound of my own thoughts? I hate this street, the unpainted windows and the dirty walls. Hate is a word I haven't used since I was a child, and now, having used it, I feel myself filling with it, feel it burning inside me. It feels good. I must be having a little madness of some sort. I don't want to hold things together any longer. Not even at home. In the words of the immortal Greta Garbo, I want to be alone. Free. Me and my servant Time.

Unobtainable, before it is too late. Christ. To have to watch yet again the great triumphal renewal of the earth as we ourselves decay. Break. I must break. My life in shreds.

'It's her first.'
'So you said.'
'Mam went with her in the ambulance. Just to give her a bit of... well you know... moral support like. Sean's in England. That's her husband. She thought she'd like to have it here. At home. I suppose you're nervous with the first one. Mam went with her. I'd say she'd be alright, wouldn't you?'
'You're to cover me. That's all you're to do.'
'I'll try and get to see her tomorrow. That is...'
'Did you hear me?'
A small girl with a dog on a lead walked past them down the hill. She walked past the gate and the parked car and then crossed the road and went into a garden on the other side. Inside the gate she stooped and let the dog free. Huge clouds were beginning to pile up in the sky. The sun was almost gone. The hedge beside them smelt sweet.
'Whose child is that?'
'How the hell would I know whose child it is!'
They turned and walked slowly towards the corner again. The man in the car put down his book and switched on the engine. Down the road a door banged. Frank groped in his pocket.
'Would you like a fag?'
'No. Did you hear what I said? You are to cover me. Nothing more. Just keep your eyes skinned.'
'I wonder will it be a boy or a girl?'
Only a golden line of sun. Rain was blowing from the west. It was going to be a stormy night.

So many wrong decisions I have made all the way down the line. I never searched for courage, never realised the possible need for it. Can I summon that neglected asset now, before it is too late? If... It's just nerves. Mary would say. The situation is getting you down. You should take a break...pull yourself together. That's what I'll do. I'll go home and have a large drink and pull myself together. Face whatever it is she has arranged for me to face. It is unkind and totally unrealistic to throw the blame on her. Face my own music. Or else I could do the other thing. He slowed down the car and pulled in to the side of the road. I could. There is nothing to stop me. I could fill the car with petrol, I could... Commitments, aged commitments. Lack of courage. Worse, of hope. They would bring me back. I would blow it. He moved back into the mainstream of traffic.

'I wouldn't mind what it was really. She'd like a wee boy. You want it to be all right. That's what really matters. You know, all right. One of my aunties had one that was... well... not quite right. That'd be always in your mind. He's grown up now. He's not too bad, just a bit soft, you know... but nice enough.'

Paining my head, all this talk. But maybe he's right, time is getting on. Maybe he's not coming.

Several large drops of rain, blown by the wind, scattered themselves on the ground. Frank ducked his head into the collar of his coat.

What did I tell you? Rain.'

Behind the clouds the sky was stained pink now.

'Red sky at night...' 'Oh, for Jesus' sake...!'

'What's up, Murphy?'

They stood for a moment and then turned their backs on the west.

'Nerves?'

Slowly they moved down the street once more. Murphy felt in his pocket for a cigarette.

'Nerves got you?'

He put the cigarette into his mouth.

'I'd say you're right. He's not coming,' he said at last.

His hand fumbled for the matches.

'It's late now. Too late.'

The car down the street revved its engine. Murphy dropped the cigarette on the ground.

'Just cover me,' he said. 'Don't do another bloody thing.'

Patrick slowed down and turned into the street. There was a car moving towards him and then past him as he swung the wheel to turn in the gate. The spring will come and then the summer. I have no energy, no will. I will put on my smile. I will resume my role. I will wait.

He became aware of the two men walking down the path towards him. Quite casually they seemed to come, the guns raised in their hands.

How strange, how very, very strange...

There was no more time.

The echoing frightened some birds, who flew uneasily into the air. Far away a dog barked. The car accelerated and was gone. It was almost dark.

from *Best Irish Short Stories 2*

 uestions

1. 'Trio' is an unusual title for this short story. Explain why you think the author chose it.
2. There are many references to the weather throughout this short story by Jennifer Johnston. Pick out three examples and say what they contribute to the story.
3. Write a character sketch of either Murphy or Frank.
4. "The way of the world, thought Murphy, one goes, another comes."
   What do you imagine Murphy meant by this?
5. From the evidence of the story what kind of person do you imagine Patrick to be?
6. Suggest a different title for this short story and explain your choice.
7. Tension plays an important part in this short story. Explain in what ways this statement is true.

➤ The Wild Duck's Nest

MICHAEL MCLAVERTY

The sun was setting, spilling gold light on the low western hills of Rathlin Island. A small boy walked jauntily along a hoof-printed path that wriggled between the folds of these hills and opened out into a crater-like valley on the cliff-top. Presently he stopped as if remembering something, then suddenly he left the path, and began running up one of the hills. When he reached the top he was out of breath and stood watching streaks of light radiating from golden-edged clouds, the scene reminding him of a picture he had seen of the Transfiguration. A short distance below him was the cow standing at the edge of a reedy lake. Colm ran down to meet her waving his stick in the air, and the

wind rumbling in his ears made him give an exultant whoop which splashed upon the hills in a shower of echoed sound. A flock of gulls lying on the short grass near the lake rose up languidly, drifting like blown snowflakes over the rim of the cliff.

The lake faced west and was fed by a stream, the drainings of the semi-circling hills. One side was open to the winds from the sea and in winter a little outlet trickled over the cliffs making a black vein in their grey sides. The boy lifted stones and began throwing them into the lake, weaving web after web on its calm surface. Then he skimmed the water with flat stones, some of them jumping the surface and coming to rest on the other side. He was delighted with himself and after listening to his echoing shouts of delight he ran to fetch his cow. Gently he tapped her on the side and reluctantly she went towards the brown-mudded path that led out of the valley. The boy was about to throw a final stone into the lake when a bird flew low over his head, its neck a-strain, and its orange-coloured legs clear in the soft light. It was a wild duck. It circled the lake twice, thrice, coming lower each time and then with a nervous flapping of wings it skidded along the surface, its legs breaking the water into a series of silvery arcs. Its wings closed, it lit silently, gave a slight shiver, and began pecking indifferently at the water.

Colm, with dilated eyes, eagerly watched it making for the farther end of the lake. It meandered between tall bulrushes, its body black and solid as stone against the greying water. Then as if it had sunk it was gone. The boy ran stealthily along the bank looking away from the lake, pretending indifference. When he came opposite to where he had last seen the bird he stopped and

33

▼

peered through the sighing reeds whose shadows streaked the water in a maze of black strokes. In front of him was a soddy islet guarded by the spears of sedge and separated from the bank by a narrow channel of water. The water wasn't too deep - he could wade across with care.

Rolling up his short trousers he began to wade, his arms outstretched, and his legs brown and stunted in the mountain water. As he drew near the islet, his feet sank in the cold mud and bubbles winked up at him. He went more carefully and nervously. Then one trouser leg fell and dipped into the water; the boy dropped his hands to roll it up, he unbalanced, made a splashing sound, and the bird arose with a squawk and whirred away over the cliffs. For a moment the boy stood frightened. Then he clambered on to the wet-soaked sod of land, which was spattered with seagulls' feathers and bits of wind-blown rushes.

Into each hummock he looked, pulling back the long grass. At last he came on the nest, facing seawards. Two flat rocks dimpled the face of the water and between them was a neck of land matted with coarse grass containing the nest. It was untidily built of dried rushes, straw and feathers, and in it lay one solitary egg. Colm was delighted. He looked around and saw no one. The nest was his. He lifted the egg, smooth and green as the sky, with a faint tinge of yellow like the reflected light from a buttercup; and then he felt he had done wrong. He put it back. He knew he shouldn't have touched it and he wondered would the bird forsake the nest. A vague sadness stole over him and he felt in his heart he had sinned. Carefully smoothing out his footprints he hurriedly left the islet and ran after his cow. The sun had now set and the cold shiver of evening enveloped him, chilling his body and saddening his mind.

In the morning he was up and away to school. He took the grass rut that edged the road for it was softer on the bare feet. His house was the last on the western headland and after a mile or so he was joined by Paddy McFall; both boys, dressed in similar hand-knitted blue jerseys and grey trousers, carried home-made school bags. Colm was full of the nest and as soon as he joined his companion he said eagerly: 'Paddy, I've a nest - a wild duck's with one egg.'

'And how do you know it's a wild duck's?' asked Paddy, slightly jealous.

'Sure I saw her with my own two eyes, her brown speckled back with a crow's patch on it, and her yellow legs -'

'Where is it?' interrupted Paddy, in a challenging tone.

'I'm not going to tell you, for you'd rob it!'

'Aach! I suppose it's a tame duck's you have or maybe an old gull's.'

Colm put out his tongue at him. 'A lot you know!' he said, 'for a gull's egg has spots and this one is greenish-white, for I had it in my hand.'

And then the words he didn't want to hear rushed from Paddy in a mocking chant, 'You had it in your hand!... She'll forsake it! She'll forsake it! She'll forsake it!' he said, skipping along the road before him.

Colm felt as if he would choke or cry with vexation.

His mind told him that Paddy was right, but somehow he couldn't give in to it and he replied: 'She'll not forsake it! She'll not! I know she'll not.'

But in school his faith wavered. Through the windows he could see moving sheets of rain - rain that dribbled down the panes filling his mind with thoughts of the lake creased and chilled by wind; the nest sodden and black with wetness; and the egg cold as a cave stone. He shivered from the thoughts and fidgeted with the inkwell cover, sliding it backwards and forwards mechanically. The mischievous look had gone from his eyes and the school day dragged on interminably. But at last they were out in the rain, Colm rushing home as fast as he could.

He was no time at all at his dinner of potatoes and salted fish until he was out in the valley now smoky with drifts of slanting rain. Opposite the islet he entered the water. The wind was blowing into his face, rustling noisily the rushes heavy with the dust of rain. A moss-cheeper, swaying on a reed like a mouse, filled the air with light cries of loneliness.

The boy reached the islet, his heart thumping with excitement, wondering did the bird forsake. He went slowly, quietly, on to the strip of land that led to the nest. He rose on his toes, looking over the ledge to see if he could see her. And then every muscle tautened. She was on, her shoulders hunched up, and her bill lying on her breast as if she were asleep. Colm's heart hammered wildly in his ears. She hadn't forsaken. He was about to turn stealthily away. Something happened. The bird moved, her neck straightened, twitching nervously from side to side. The boy's head swam with lightness. He stood transfixed. The wild duck with a panicky flapping, rose heavily, and flew off towards the sea...A guilty silence enveloped the boy...He turned to go away, hesitated, and glanced back at the bare nest; it'd be no harm to have a look. Timidly he approached it, standing straight, and gazing over the edge. There in the nest lay two eggs. He drew in his breath with delight, splashing quickly from the island, and ran off whistling in the rain.

Questions

1 It is obvious that Colm, the boy in this story has a great love for nature and the countryside. Explain by reference to the text why this is so.

2 What evidence is there in the story to suggest that Colm's family was not well off?

3 'A vague sadness stole over him and he felt in his heart he had sinned'. Explain, using your own words, why the boy felt this way.

4 What are your feelings towards the boy after he lifts the wild duck's egg? Explain your answer.

5 There is tension in the story once his friend Paddy says 'She'll forsake it! She'll forsake it!' How does the author create this tension?

6 The author Michael McLaverty has a keen eye for descriptive detail. Pick out some descriptions which you particularly like and give reasons for your choice.

UNIT 1

READING

➤ The lodge

Stephen walked slowly up the hill towards the trees. He had promised his science teacher that day that on his way home from school he would collect samples of leaves for the next day's lesson.

He reached the edge of the wood and checked which leaves he needed from the list which Mr Benson had given him. He worked quickly, putting the leaves in a plastic carrier bag and ticking off his list. The first drops of rain fell just as he had completed his collection. Stephen glanced at his watch and decided that if he sheltered for about fifteen minutes, he could just about make it home in time for tea and the heavy shower would probably be over by then. His mother would be furious if he was soaked but she would worry if he was late.

He looked around and decided that his best bet would be to make a run for the old Lodge and perhaps squeeze himself into the porch to keep dry. No one had lived in the Lodge for years. The windows were boarded up and the building itself was in a pretty bad state. Stephen remembered that some older boys from his school had been hurt when they had fallen through the rotten roof timbers. That had been about a year ago, but no one had really played around the Lodge since then.

He leaned heavily on the door and was surprised to find that it moved about five centimetres. The locks had given way in the rotten wood. He gave the door a push and it opened enough to let him squeeze through the space into a narrow hallway.

The place was in a real mess – the stairs were in front of him, but he could see by the light from the doorway that they would not be safe to walk on, as some of the steps were missing and the banister was broken. He pushed open the door on his left. Stephen could see that there was light coming in between the boards on the windows, and when his eyes got used to the gloom, he could make out an old fireplace on the far wall. He was examining this when he heard a sort of dry cough behind him. He suddenly felt scared and wondered if he would get into trouble for being inside the Lodge. His mouth felt dry and he stumbled over his words - 'I'm just waiting here until the rain stops – I'm not doing any harm.'

A tall, middle-aged man was standing in the doorway. He was looking at Stephen in a strange way. Stephen wondered if he was one of the managers from the big farm on the other side of the woods.

The man at first said nothing. His clothes were a bit odd. He wore a tweed jacket and the sort of trousers which gamekeepers wear. Stephen hadn't seen that sort of suit before. He decided that the man must be from the farm.

Just then, the alarm on Stephen's watch made its bleeping noise – he had set it for tea-time. The man spoke: 'What is that?'

'It's only my watch,' said Stephen. 'It's new and it gives the day and date and it's a stopwatch and it has an alarm. It can play a tune if I press this button.' He touched his watch and the electronic tune played. The man stared at it in silence.

Stephen started moving towards the door, still a bit worried. The man did not try to stop him, so he pushed his way through the door, squeezed out of the outside door and, holding his carrier bag tightly, ran down the hill.

He had been really scared but he had no need to be – he hadn't been doing any damage and he had only squeezed in through a gap that had more or less been there. That was it – the gap – he had just managed to squeeze out again, so which way had the man come in?

'You're a bit late, Stephen,' said his mum. 'Did you get caught in the rain?'

'No, I'm OK Mum,' he called from the hall. 'I managed to shelter.'

He sat down at the table and started to butter his bread.

'Where did you shelter, love?' said his mum.

'In the old Lodge.'

'Oh Stephen, you know I don't like you going up there – not after the other lads were hurt. Anyway, I know it's only an old local tale but the place is supposed to be haunted and I know that's silly, but, to be honest, I still don't like the idea of your being there – the ghost of Colonel Latimer might not like you ....'

Questions

1 What was Stephen doing in the woods?
2 For how long had the lodge been vacant?
3 What made Stephen think that the man was from the farm?
4 Give two reasons why you think Stephen ran down the hill.
5 Did Stephen's mother like him being in the Lodge? Explain why.
6 Choose a different title for the story and give reasons for your choice.
7 How does the story make you feel?

POETRY

➤ To my grown-up son

My hands were busy through the day,
I didn't have much time to play
The little games you asked me to,
I didn't have much time for you.
I'd wash your clothes; I'd sew and cook,
But when you'd bring your picture book
And ask me, please, to share your fun,
I'd say, 'A little later, son.'

I'd tuck you in all safe at night,
And hear your prayers, turn out the light,
Then tiptoe softly to the door,
I wish I'd stayed a minute more.

For life is short, and years rush past,
A little boy grows up so fast,
No longer is he at your side,
His precious secrets to confide.

The picture books are put away,
There are no children's games to play,
No good night kiss, no prayers to hear,
That all belongs to yesteryear.

My hands once busy, now lie still,
The days are long and hard to fill,
I wish I might go back and do,
The little things you asked me to.

Alice E. Chase

Questions

1   Which of the boy's parents is speaking in this poem? Give reasons for your answer.
2   Why does the parent regret not having spent more time with the boy?
3   Describe the kind of feelings that this poem gives you.
4   Do you think that this poem paints a true picture of life? Why?
5   Pick out some words or phrases from the poem and say why you like them.

1 Where do you think this photograph was taken?
2 You have been asked to suggest a suitable title for the picture, using just one word. What word would you choose? Why?
3 Write a short account of what you think the girl is thinking at that particular moment.

HARD ROCK TODAY. HARD OF HEARING TOMORROW?

A sharp stereo can sound pretty dull if you get a build up of earwax. Don't turn the volume up. Turn to Earex instead. It helps clear unwanted earwax. No problem. It won't show and it could save the discomfort of syringing. When earwax leaves you hard of hearing, Earex will upgrade your stereo for under £2.

Clearer ears for sharper hearing

1 In what way does this advertisement attract your attention?
2 At whom is this advertisement aimed?
3 What are the advantages of the product according to the manufacturer?
4 Do you think the caption in bold print could be true? Why?

☐ PERSONAL AND FUNCTIONAL WRITING

1 Your father has changed his job and consequently you have moved to a new town. Write a **letter** to your best friend in which you describe how you feel about the change. Mention some details of your new house, the town, your new school, etc.

2 Write a **short story** beginning with the words:
   Suddenly the lights went out ...

3 Write a **composition** on one of the following titles:
   (a) How the aeroplane has changed our lives.
   (b) The Olympic Games
   (c) A wet day
   (d) My kind of music

1   Punctuate the following passage:
    excuse me mr ryan my mother wants to know if youll have fresh vegetables
    on wednesday yes we will john and ill keep some for her

2   Correct one error in each of the following:
    (a) Their is no place like home.
    (b) The tied rises twice each day.
    (c) We begun to laugh out loud.

3   Write out in your copy the correct words for the spaces below:

big	bigger	biggest
great	_____	_____
far	_____	_____
bad	_____	_____
beautiful	_____	_____
good	_____	_____
many	_____	_____
little	_____	_____
handsome	_____	_____

4   Complete the following sentences using either 'its' or 'it's'.
    (a) ____ too cold to go fishing today.
    (b) Money sometimes loses ____ value.
    (c) ____ coat is striped and ____ like a horse.
    (d) ____ a shame that you lost the match.
    (e) When a cat is angry ____ back is arched.
    (f) ____ not fair that you were blamed.

5   Write a sentence showing the proper use of each of the following.

grown	cereal	plain	stake	real
groan	serial	plane	steak	reel

bare	waste	night	foul	flower
bear	waist	knight	fowl	flour

UNIT 2

READING

➤ **First day at school**

The morning came, without any warning, when my sisters surrounded me, wrapped me in scarves, tied up my bootlaces, thrust a cap on my head, and stuffed a baked potato in my pocket.

'What's this?' I said.

'You're starting school today.'

'I ain't. I'm stopping 'ome.'

'Now, come on, Loll. You're a big boy now.'

'I ain't.'

'You are.'

'Boo-hoo.'

They picked me up bodily, kicking and bawling, and carried me up to the road.

'Boys who don't go to school get put into boxes, and turn into rabbits, and get chopped up on Sundays.'

I felt this was overdoing it rather, but I said no more after that. I arrived at the school just three feet tall and fatly wrapped in my scarves. The playground roared like a rodeo, and the potato burned through my thigh. Old boots, ragged stockings, torn trousers and skirts, went skating and skidding around me. The rabble closed in; I was encircled; grit flew in my face like shrapnel. Tall girls with frizzled hair, and huge boys with sharp elbows, began to prod me with interest. They plucked at my scarves, spun me round like a top, screwed my nose, and stole my potato.

I was rescued at last by a gracious lady – the sixteen-year-old junior teacher – who boxed a few ears and dried my face and led me off to The Infants. I spent the first day picking holes in paper, then went home in a smouldering temper.

'What's the matter, Loll? Didn't he like it at school then?'

'They never gave me the present!'

'Present? What present?'

'They said they'd give me a present.'

'Well, now, I'm sure they didn't.'

'They did! They said: 'You're Laurie Lee, ain't you? Well, just you sit there for the present.' I sat there all day but I never got it. I ain't going back there again!'

But after a week I felt like a veteran and grew as ruthless as anyone else. Somebody had stolen my baked potato, so I swiped somebody else's apple.

Laurie Lee *Cider with Rosie*

Questions

1   How did the young boy feel about starting school?
2   Why was the young boy in a smouldering temper?
3   What does the phrase 'felt like a veteran' mean?
4   Do you think that all the schoolchildren were from well-off families?
5   Find four words used to describe the actions of the other children when the boy arrived at school.
6   What picture comes to mind when you read each of the following expressions?
      'fatly wrapped in my scarves'
      'the playground roared like a rodeo'.
      'The rabble closed in'.
7   Can you remember your first day at school? Describe your experiences briefly.

WHAT I HAVE READ

- Choose a **poem** that you have studied in which the poet refers to his youth or to times gone by.
- Give the title of the poem and say who wrote it.
- Give the story of the poem in your own words.
- Quote four lines from the poem.
- Give two reasons why you like or dislike the poem you have chosen.

1   You have been bitten by a savage dog owned by a local farmer. Write a **letter** of complaint. Here are some hints:
Crossing a field....minding my own business....going fishing to river....loud barks....run....try to defend myself....broken fishing-rod....pants torn....leg gashed....saved by neighbour....visit to doctor....still out of school....suggest action about dog

2   You have witnessed a road accident in which a young boy/girl was knocked down by a hit-and-run driver. The police have asked you for details of what you saw. Write a **report** of the incident giving as much information as you can.

3   Write a **composition** on one of the following titles.
(a) A punishment well deserved   (c) My choice of career
(b) The day nothing went right for me   (d) Teachers

GRAMMAR

1   Punctuate the following passage:
i live near here he said and i have many friends in sarsfield avenue however its very quiet at the moment because theyre on holidays

2   List the following words in alphabetical order:
common, playful, summer, bicycle, foreign, loyal, distant, ground, happy, vexed.

3   Correct one error in each of the following:
(a) The criminal will be hung tomorrow.
(b) Have either of you lost a watch?
(c) First prize was a check for fifty pounds.

4   Write out these sentences in your copy filling in the missing words.
A ____ is a stringed instrument which is the symbol of Ireland.
Words in large print at the top of a newspaper or magazine are ____.
A ____ is a building where things are made by machinery.
The cutting edge of a weapon is a ____.
A ____ is a boat for rescuing people at sea.
A ____ is a young lion, young fox or young bear.

5   Spelling test

captain	sketch	bargain	assistant	quality
poison	title	quantity	station	responsible
disaster	afternoon	million	whispered	breakfast

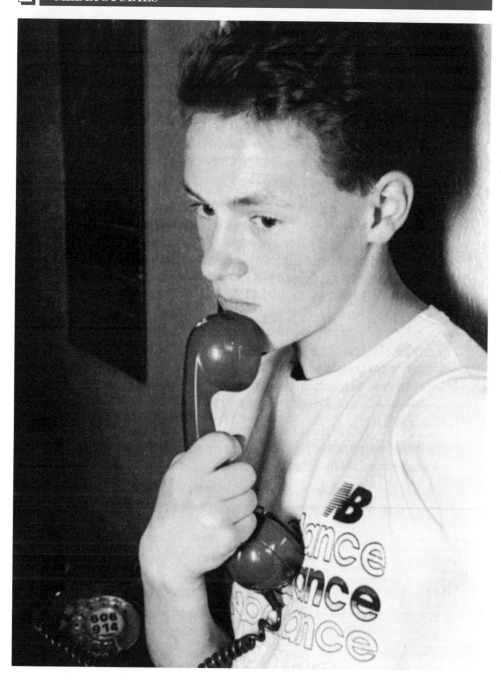

1   Where do you think this picture was taken? Why?
2   Suggest a suitable caption for this picture and give reasons for your choice.
3   How would you describe the expression on the young man's face?
4   Write a short account of what is happening in this picture from the point of
    view of the young man.

NOW, A TELEVISION THAT BREAKS THE SOUND BARRIER

The launch of Black Diamond television technology saw Mitsubishi unveil the sharpest, clearest television picture the world had ever seen.

Now, to complement the perfect picture, comes the ultimate in television sound.

Mitsubishi Black Diamond NICAM Stereo Sound.

A sound so incredible, you won't believe your ears.

A massive 40 watts of built-in speaker power, up to eight times more dynamic than most conventional televisions, transforms everything you watch into a live performance.

So all your favourite programmes take on a new life.

Rented movies are played back in full living stereo.

And, as all Mitsubishi Black Diamond NICAM Stereo Sound televisions are fitted with

a built-in decoder to receive NICAM stereo broadcasts, they're ready now for the future.

Your listening pleasure is further enhanced as some of the New Generation Black Diamond televisions also boast a remote controlled swivel base, to bring you face to face with the most incredible sound and picture experience – wherever you're sitting.

There's even a special AV Memory Setting to let you programme the sound to suit anything you watch.

While an on-screen graphic equalizer allows you to fine tune the sound at the push of a button.

And talk about speaker systems!

The new Mitsubishi Black Diamond range features four impressive sound systems from double drive and acoustic turbo speakers to 3-D and bass reflex speakers.

Check the Golden Pages for the Mitsubishi Centre nearest you where you can see (and hear) the amazing New Generation Black Diamond Range.

At last, a television that sounds as good as it looks.

MITSUBISHI *Black Diamond* NICAM STEREO SOUND

1   What feature of this advertisement is the most striking in your opinion? Explain why?
2   In what ways does the advertisement try to persuade you to buy the product?
3   The props play an important part in this advertisement. Explain this statement.
4   Comment on the effectiveness of the copy (written part) of this advertisement.

UNIT 3

READING

➤ Everest at last!

The ridge continued as before. Giant cornices on the right, steep rock slopes on the left. I went on cutting steps on the narrow strip of snow. The ridge curved away to the right and we had no idea where the top was. As I cut around the back of one hump, another higher one would swing into view. Time was passing and the ridge seemed never-ending. I was beginning to tire a little now. I had been cutting steps continuously for two hours, and Tenzing, too, was moving very slowly. As I chipped steps around still another corner, I wondered rather dully just how long we could keep it up. Our original zest had now quite gone and it was turning more into a grim struggle. I then realised that the ridge ahead, instead of still monotonously rising, now dropped sharply away, and far below I could see the North Col and the Rongbuk glacier. I looked upwards to see a narrow snow ridge running up to a snowy summit. A few more whacks of the ice-axe in the firm snow and we stood on top.

My initial feelings were of relief – relief that there were no more steps to cut – no more ridges to traverse and no more humps to tantalise us with hopes of success. I looked at Tenzing and, in spite of the balaclava, goggles and oxygen mask all encrusted with long icicles that concealed his face, there was no disguising his infectious grin of pure delight as he looked all around him. We shook hands and then Tenzing threw his arm around my shoulders and we thumped each other on the back until we were almost breathless. It was 11.30 a.m. The ridge had taken us two and a half hours, but it seemed like a lifetime. I turned off the oxygen and removed my set. I had carried my camera, loaded with colour film, inside my shirt to keep it warm, so I now produced it and got Tenzing to pose on top for me, waving his axe on which was a string of flags – United Nations, British, Nepalese and Indian. Then I turned my attention to the great stretch of country lying below us in every direction.

Sir Edmund Hillary

uestions

1   Why could the climbers not see the top of the mountain?
2. Why did they thump each other on the back?
5   Write down three facts given in the story which prove that Hillary and Tenzing were climbing in a very cold region.
6   Why do you think that Hillary turned off the oxygen and removed his set?
7   Look up the following difficult words in your dictionary and use each one in a sentence of your own:
    traverse   tantalise   encrusted   infectious
8   Imagine that you were with Hillary and Tenzing on the summit. Describe your feelings.

POETRY
....

➤ The weaker sex
'Open the jar of Pickles.'
I hear my mother cry
I jump up with enthusiasm
And race to where they lie
'I'll do it,' says my father, full of power
I protest endlessly and seize the jar
My hand fearlessly grips the metal top
And freezes into a confident lock
I stare knowingly at my father who stares back
simmering with laughter.

I turn the lid this way, I turn it that
My bones crunch with strain
but my hand slides on my sweat
By now my father has exploded with laughter
'You women!' he chuckles and sighs
I flush with embarrassment and screw up my eyes
My mind curses the jar
'Who likes them anyway?' I ask, not with anger
'We all do!' replies my mother.

The fight continued
I pleaded with it for ever so long
'You'll never do it, you're not strong!'
How could I prove to Dad he was wrong?
My hands were throbbing with pain
'Look, give it to me!'
A pair of large hands attacked me, in vain!
I screamed in my head
'I'm not giving in!'

The onions must have heard me
For all of a sudden the lid gave a spin
And opened in my hand
'We're quite strong, us women!'
I announced with pride.
So all you female jar wrestlers
when you fell like giving up
Remember my victory.

                    Wendy Richmond

Questions

1   The poet's father 'has exploded with laughter'. Why?
2   What do you think her father means when he exclaims 'you women!'?
3   Suggest another title for this poem and say why you chose it.
4   What lesson can be learned from the poem?
5   What is the tone of the poem? Support your answer by quoting from the poem.

1 Who is being targeted in this advertisement?
2 What strikes you first when you look at this advertisement?
3 Comment on the effectiveness of the caption.
4 The artist focuses our attention on the mint which is in the form of a
   measuring tape. Explain why you think she does this.

DREAM NO MORE

Ducatis have always been the stuff of dreams. That's hardly surprising. Their subtle blend of performance and elegance, so highly desirable, is rarely encountered.

Some dreams, thankfully, can come true. Our increasingly competitive pricing policy makes a Ducati more affordable than ever. And the new SS series comprises a range of models that are more alluring than ever. Full of character, with power and handling to put you in total control. Plus the reassurance of The Ducati Assistance, 24 month unlimited mileage factory warranty and 12 months RAC cover.

So if you're still dreaming of a Ducati, it's time you pinched yourself - and woke up to reality. There's so much more to find out, so to get the whole story contact Ducati Information Services now.

DUCATI

Hotline 0480 436383 24 hours/7 days   Ref:MCI2SS
Ducati Information Services, Spitfire Close,
Ermine Business Park, Huntingdon, Cambs PE18 6XY.

Prices are correct at time of going to press and include VAT but exclude on the road extras at £250.

600SS Ducati Red
£5,400

750SS Ducati Red
£6,200

900SS Ducati Red
£7,600

900SL Ferrari Yellow
£8,000

1   Where would you expect to find this advertisement? Make a list of where we find advertisements e.g. magazines, newspapers.
2   What overall impression does this advertisement try to convey?
3   Which feature of the advertisement is the most striking in your opinion? Why?
4   Why do you think so much advertising revenue is spent on advertisements in newspapers and magazines?

1   Write a **letter** inviting your foreign penfriend to visit Ireland. You should try to make the country sound as interesting as possible. Here are some hints:
next month....school holidays....meet at airport....home by car....own room....near beach....father's boat....sea fishing....wonderful scenery....mountain climbing....visits to city....cinemas....theatres.... restaurants....looking forward to visit.

2   Write a **story** about how you and a friend had an amusing adventure. It need not be true. Begin like this:
I still laugh when I think about it. It all began when ....

3   Write a **composition** on one of the following titles.
An adventure at sea
Working on a farm
Famous inventions
Childhood memories

GRAMMAR

1   Write the following out properly
my name is robert martin i am twelve years old i live with my parents at willow avenue my father is a policeman he spends his days in the streets of dublin

2   Write out in your copy the feminine of the following nouns:

actor	hero	lion	nephew	waiter
stallion	bachelor	manager	duke	landlord

3   Correct the following sentences by putting in apostrophes:
(a) The girls book was on her desk.
(b) We noticed that the womans hand was bleeding.
(c) My mothers purse was stolen by our neighbours son.
(d) The childrens clothes are in their parents car.
(e) The boys schoolbags are in the classroom.

4   Explain each of the following expressions by using them properly in a sentence:
at loggerheads
make no bones about it
throw in the towel
have a crow to pluck with
sit on the fence
take French leave
kick over the traces
rub the wrong way

UNIT
4

READING

➤ Slaves to TV

Are you a slave to television? More importantly – are you harming your children by encouraging them to watch television from their earliest years?
  Consider these research findings:

- Two out of three schoolchildren watch three to five hours a day. Over a year, that is more than the time they spend in school.

- In one survey, out of 5,000 children between 6 and 11 interviewed, only three had no TV at home and only six did not watch regularly. Only two per cent of those over seven had not watched a late-night movie. From the age of nine most children watch TV regularly until midnight.

- Three to five-year-olds are probably among the heaviest viewers of all. In America they found toddlers were glued to the box for up to 54 hours a week and there's no reason to think our under-fives watch less.
    It's easy to see why parents encourage children to watch TV from an early age – it keeps them quiet.
    And in tele-addicted households, real-life events take second place to TV. Meals are eaten on trays in front of the television and talking, visits from friends or going out have to be slotted in around favourite programmes.

The TV Action Group, formed five years ago by worried parents and teachers, collected information on the effects of watching TV and warned parents of the dangers.

The group points out that watching television transforms children from their normal active, playful selves to a trance-like state, after which they are often irritable.

Because it is so undemanding, watching TV can be addictive and parents, afraid of rows, let the child decide how much to watch.

Young children who watch too much TV are often slower to speak and have poor vocabularies. The physical brain strain of converting TV's lines and dots into a meaningful picture is considerable. Together with lack of eye movement, this can produce anxiety, sleeplessness, nightmares, headaches, perceptual disorders, poor concentration and blunted senses.

The group even goes so far as to say that TV can hinder brain development and that seeing violence encourages children to imitate the same behaviour.

Over the years there has been a mountain of research on the subject and for almost every argument it is possible to produce a counter-claim. But after sifting through some of the evidence and talking to a variety of experts, it is possible to draw up some commonsense guidelines for parents. The first is that it is *not* good for children – especially young children – to watch too much television. How much harm it does them depends entirely on the child and the kind of home they have.

All other guidelines are secondary to this.

Questions

1 What age group watches the greatest amount of television?
2 How is the family routine influenced by television watching?
3 How are children affected by watching too much television?
4 Do you think that children should be allowed to watch television during the school week?
5 Name your favourite television programme and say why you like it.
7 Have you ever been strongly influenced by what you saw on television? Pick one example and write briefly about it.
6 'The world is an open book due to television.'
   Do you agree or disagree with this statement. Why?

WHAT I HAVE READ

- Give an account of a **short story**, which you have read, that deals with an incident from the life of a young boy or girl.
- Do you think that the incident described in the story of your choice was true-to-life? Give reasons for your answer.

1 Select an appropriate title for this picture and explain your choice.
2 Where do you think this picture was taken? Why?
3 How would you describe the expression on the children's faces?
4 Write a short story based on this picture.

How long does it take to read the ingredients on a butter wrapper?

As long as it takes to say 100% natural.

Butter.
Often copied, never equalled.

ndc

1 Suggest five reasons why you think this is or is not an effective advertisement.
2 What is the key phrase in this advertisement? Explain you choice.
3 Suggest some ways by which you think the advertisement might be improved.
4 Describe the design of the National Dairy Council logo. How suitable do you consider it? Why?

1 Write a **letter** in reply to the following advertisement in the newspaper.

> '**Required:** second-hand motorcycle in good condition. Reply, giving full details to Box 166 *The Evening Press*'.

2 **I'll never forget**

What has happened to you that you will never forget? Think back over your life and recall the events that stand out in your memory. They may be small, trivial incidents or unusual or dramatic ones. They may be pleasant or unpleasant. We all have memories that stand out in our minds and sometimes we don't know why they keep coming back.

Write an **account** of something you will never forget.

3 Write a **composition** on one of the following titles:
   (a) People who annoy me
   (b) Fishing is a splendid pastime
   (c) How I hate the alarm clock
   (d) A school tour

GRAMMAR

1 Insert the correct word in each of the following sentences.
   The weather is far (to, two, too) mild for snow.
   The old man fell (of, off) the ladder.
   The thief is guilty (to, of, by) a crime.
   Napoleon led the invasion (to, of, by) Russia.
   The teacher was vexed (at, with) the child.
   You should be ashamed (of, at) what you did.

2 Punctuate the following passage.
   twelve years ago when paul was eighteen years old he joined aer lingus the irish airline he spent four years training to be a pilot now he is thirty years old and he flies a jumbo jet from dublin to new york

3 Spelling test

chimney	forehead	chocolate	mattress	niece
sandwich	relation	cellar	seller	parlour
costume	engineer	carriage	traveller	butcher
aeroplane	plumber	vehicle	island	harbour

4 What sounds do the following suggest to you?

brakes	telephone	drum	whip	wind
cork	clock	donkey	frog	horse
pig	owl	lion	duck	bee

5 Describe in one sentence, the occupations of the following:
   chemist, porter, barrister, chef, ambassador, architect, cashier, dentist, engineer, coxswain.

UNIT 5

READING

➤ A secret past

Grandmother was very strait-laced. She wasn't at all like the fairy-tale Grannies you read of in books. She never laughed, and I rarely saw her smile. She was kind to me, but never seemed very interested in what I did. When we went for tea, she sat upright on a straight-backed chair. I used to feel nervous about crumbs and spills. I always felt that she was rather like the furniture in her rather dark house – very old fashioned and respectable, dark and gloomy, and built to last. Both the furniture and Grandmother made me feel small and cramped, as if I couldn't be me in her house.

My ideas about Grandmother underwent a drastic change when I was about twelve. That was when her old friend, May Cooper, came to stay with her.

The day I overheard Grandmother giggling – yes, giggling – I realised there was more to her than I had ever guessed. For the first time I was curious. I resolved to ask my mother about her childhood when I got a chance.

'Grandmother laughed today,' I said. 'I've never heard her laugh before. She sounded so young. She's always seemed so old and sad to me.'

'I suppose you only know her as an old woman,' my mother said. 'She's aged a lot since your Grandfather died. What a pity you can't remember him. He was devoted to her.'

'He wasn't your real father, though, was he?'

'No, but I always wished he had been. I would have liked a father like him,' said my mother sadly.

'What happened to your real father?' I asked.

'I don't know. Your grandmother never talked about it. I gather he died after I was born. Mother must have married again, but I don't know how long after. My earliest memories include them both. I always called him Father.'

Grandmother and May Cooper came to tea the next day. May was a bright, lively, chatty sort of woman. She wore a red skirt and a yellow cardigan. Her lips were orange, her eye-lids blue and her hair an unnatural reddish-brown.

Seeing May next to Grandmother, who was in her dark wool suit, I wondered what on earth they had in common.

'Have you and Grandmother been friends for a long time?' I asked May.

'Dearie me, yes,' laughed May. 'We worked the theatres together.

'Theatres?' I couldn't believe it. Grandmother on the stage? Perhaps she had been a serious actress – or a wardrobe mistress. Yes, that was more like it.

'We were in the chorus line together!' May chuckled. 'Do you recall those feathers, Agnes? Do you remember when we were appearing in Newcastle?' and May collapsed in laughter. To my surprise, Grandmother joined in. Then she said,

'Let's not let too many secrets out of the bag, May!'

'Was Grandmother trying to keep May quiet, do you think?' I asked Mother later. 'I didn't know she worked in the theatre. When was that?'

'It was before she was married. I don't ever remember her talking about it to us. I just picked things up from the odd thing May said, and from Father. I gather she was the youngest of ten children. her parents were well off, but distant and remote. They had a nanny and servants to look after them. When she was only four, her mother died, and her father soon after. From then on she was passed round the family from brother to sister like a parcel. I gather they treated her like an unpaid servant, she had to scrub and clean and look after her nieces and nephews, and never knew anything she could call home.

When she was eighteen she ran away, and somehow or other went on the stage. I believe she sent a photo back to the oldest brother after six months, of herself dressed as a chorus girl. The brother was shocked, and wrote and told her the family never wanted to see her as long as she lived. She had let down the family name.'

'What a sad story,' I said. 'Did she never see any of her family again?'

'No, I don't think so,' said my mother. 'I remember when I was small, being sent to the country. I had been ill, and my mother was told I wouldn't get better if I didn't get out of the city. so she swallowed her pride and wrote and asked if I could stay with them. I stayed in the lodge with the gamekeeper and his wife, and only dimly remember the big house, which of course I only saw from a distance. I don't even know where it was.'

The next day, early in the morning, we got a phone call from May. Grandmother had died in her sleep.

After the funeral, I heard May ask my mother if she could talk to her. They went off up to the guest room where May had been staying. When she reappeared, my mother's eyes were red, but she seemed happier. I couldn't understand it.

Questions

1   Why did the child feel nervous when visiting her grandmother's house?
2   What effect did the giggling have on the child?
3   What do May's clothes and appearance say about her as a person?
4   What can you tell about the grandmother's character from this extract?
5   Why do you think the grandmother chose a straight-backed chair?
6   Suggest reasons why the grandmother did not want to talk about her first marriage.
7   Why do you suppose she sent a photograph to her oldest brother?
8   Why do you think the daughter had to stay in the lodge with the gamekeeper and his wife?
9   This extract ends just as the grandmother's secret past is about to be revealed. How do you imagine the story ended. Give your reasons.

POETRY

> ## Cold feet

They have all gone across
They are all turning to see
They are all shouting 'Come on'
They are all waiting for me.

I look through the gaps in the footway
And my heart shrivels with fear,
For way below the river is flowing
So quick and so cold and so clear.

And all that there is between it
And me falling down there is this:
A few wooden planks (not very thick)
And between each, a little abyss.

The holes get right under my sandals,
I can see straight through to the rocks,
And if I don't look, I can feel it,
Just there, through my shoes and my socks.

Suppose my feet and my legs withered up
And slipped through the slats like a rug;
Suppose I suddenly went very thin
Like that baby that slid down the plug?

I know that it cannot happen,
But suppose that it did, what then?
Would they be able to find me
And take me back home again?

They have all gone across
They are waiting to see
They are all shouting 'Come on'
But they'll have to carry me.

Brian Lee

Questions

1   Who do you think is waiting on the other side of the footbridge?
2   Why does the child suddenly become frightened?
3   Would he feel less frightened if he closed his eyes?
4   Have you ever had cold feet? Describe briefly the circumstances.

1   Pick a suitable title for the picture and say why you chose it.
2   What do you think is happening in the background of the picture? Give
    your reasons.
3   Look at the two old men in the picture and write an imaginary dialogue
    between them.

1 Make out the text of an advertisement which you would use to sell Statoil products.
2 Are there any other features which you think would improve this advertisement, keeping in mind the target audience?
3 Comment on the design of the company logo.
4 Why do many advertisements have small print at the bottom?

1   You are a young American girl/boy staying with relatives in the West of Ireland. Write a **postcard** to your parents telling them about your stay. Include the following ideas:
arrival....welcome....countryside....weather....food.... activities.

2   Write a **short story** beginning with the words:
'We must be out of petrol', said John.

3   Write a **composition** on one of the following titles:
(a) Buying a new bicycle
(b) Life in the year 2000
(c) My favourite pastimes
(d) The life of a schoolboy/schoolgirl

GRAMMAR

1   Punctuate the following passage:
have you got a colour television asked the inspector yes replied the girl have you a proper licence asked the inspector i dont know replied the girl im only the babysitter

2   Give the short form of the following, using an apostrophe:

could not	she will	you are	I would
have not	we have	did not	I am
it is	do not		

Put each example of the short form in a simple sentence.

3   Correct one error in each of the following:
(a) That storey is absolutely true.
(b) Most of the people likes television.
(c) A pack of hounds were chasing the fox.

4   Re-write the following passage beginning with the words 'John said that' and make any changes that are necessary.
Yesterday, I went home from school and did my homework. Then my friends called and we all went to the pictures. My father gave me fifty pence to spend on myself. I came home at 11.00 o'clock. I stayed up late because I had no school today.

UNIT 6

READING

➤ The scout

The field on the outskirts of the town was deserted. Before the flash and what looked like a tube of dust particles, there were birds in the trees and a couple of horses stood near the white fence. The birds suddenly became quiet and flew off and the horses gave a high whinny, rolled their eyes until the whites showed, and galloped off to the farthest end of the field. There was a low rumbling then the silver, blinding flash and the whirling dust like a finger pointing to the ground, reached down to the grass. The dry blades crackled and scorched at the rim of the dust column. The cloud settled and a young man looked out of the mist at the field around him. He was tall and slim with pale, smooth skin and bright blue piercing eyes. His fair hair was short and brushed straight back from his forehead. He wore light coloured trousers and a plain sweater and looked unsteady on his feet. He leaned down and lightly touched the grass, placed his feet more firmly on the slightly muddy ground and fumbled with some buttons on his large black watch. He stood more confidently and then walked quickly towards the fence.

He stopped for a moment at the path, lifted his head and seemed to listen, then turned abruptly to his right and strode down the lane until he reached the road.

About two kilometres down the road a

truck was driving along, the driver whistling and looking forward to reaching home that evening. He wound down the window and leaned his elbow on the sill. Another ten kilometres or so of country roads and he would be on the outskirts of town.

He sat up straight in his seat and concentrated on the engine noise. He was sure he had felt the engine speed up. He lifted his foot from the accelerator but seemed to maintain his speed. He felt a cold sweat break out on his forehead and his hand moved towards the air brake lever and rested just above it. He shook his head, scanned the dials on the dashboard and told himself that his imagination was playing tricks on him. He continued to check the gauges and strained to listen to any change in the engine noise for about a kilometre and a half. Then he began to relax. 'You're losing your nerve for the road.' he told himself as he rubbed his hand over his eyes and wiped away the sweat with the back of his hand.

He saw the young hitch-hiker standing by the fence at the side of the field and applied his brakes. The man looked out of place there in his smart, well-cut clothes, but he seemed respectable and the driver was ready for some company. It would break the rest of the journey and maybe stop his mind playing these silly tricks.

He held open the cab door and the young man got in. He said nothing and the driver released the brakes and drove off.

'Where are you headed then?' he asked. The young man touched his watch briefly and then spoke.

'I cannot tell – to the centre maybe.'

'Well, I'm going about another sixty kilometres – you can stick with me and maybe somebody will take you further south if it's the smoke you want to get to.'

'The smoke,' the young man repeated.

'You're travelling light aren't you?' asked the driver. 'Have you left your stuff somewhere?'

'Yes, but I have all I need.'

'Where you from then – you don't look like you're from these parts?'

'You wouldn't know where I've come from,' the young man said.

'Hey, I'm a long-distance driver – there aren't many places I don't know – if it has roads, I might know it.'

'You cannot know where I am from,' he said and stared straight ahead.

The lorry driver shrugged and asked, 'Are you here on business?'

'Yes I am.'

'What line are you in?'

'I am not in a line,' the man said.

The driver sighed. This bloke was hard work. He seemed like some kind of nut-case. He tried again.

'Who do you work for – what's your job, like – you know?'

There was a pause and the young man answered 'I work for my masters. They wish to know many things and I must find them out.'

'Ah, some sort of research, I see,' said the driver.

The young man then asked the driver many questions – about working, eating, sleeping, what jobs people did and how they lived.

'You some sort of foreigner?' said the driver as he answered yet another really obvious, almost stupid question.

'I may be.'

'Look, mate,' said the driver, 'I eat three meals a day, like a few pints and eight hours sleep. I have a wife and two kids and a decent home – have you got everything you want to know?'

'No, I must know many, many more things,' said the young man.

'Well, tell your masters that you run the risk of getting your pretty nose broken if you keep acting so nosey.'

The lorry swerved suddenly and jolted out of control. It spun round a tight corner and crashed into a fence at the side of the road. The driver's head hit the screen and he slumped unconscious over the wheel. A trickle of blood from a cut ran down the side of his cheek.

The young man reached out, touched the blood and looked at the red liquid on his fingers. He pulled up the sleeve of his sweater and found a gash on his arm just below his elbow.

From the gash, some wires stuck out. He pushed the wires into the tear and pulled down his sleeve.

He opened the cab door, jumped down and walked off down the road.

Questions

1 Why did the peaceful country scene suddenly change?
2 What prompted the driver to stop for the hitch-hiker?
3 What does the phrase 'the smoke' mean?
4 Where do you think the young man had come from?
5 Why, in your opinion, did the engine suddenly speed up?
6 Why do you think the driver lost control of the truck?
7 What happened next? Write two paragraphs explaining what you think might have happened.

WHAT I HAVE READ

- Give the name and author of any **novel** you have read which deals with the adventures of boys or girls.
- Describe briefly the setting and explain its importance to the story.
- Select one character from the novel whom you particularly liked and explain why?

1 Your home is situated near the local disco club. Write a **letter** to the manager complaining about the constant noise late at night.

2 Write an **account** of a fire, using the words below:
   walking in town....late at night....smell of smoke....screams....face at window....phone....police....fire brigade....rescue....newspaper report....you are a hero.

3 Write a **composition** on one of the following titles
   (a) Monday morning in our house   (c) Exploring an uninhabited island
   (b) My funniest memory   (d) The life of an airline pilot

GRAMMAR

1 Write out the following list of words and write the correct words in the spaces:

   I sell   I sold   I have sold
   I eat   _____   _____
   I catch   _____   _____
   I fight   _____   _____
   I blow   _____   _____
   I draw   _____   _____
   I do   _____   _____
   I drive   _____   _____
   I fly   _____   _____

2 Punctuate the following passage:
   paul omeara was my best friend at st michaels college we both were very good at english irish and french now hes an important official in washington

3 Write sentences showing the proper use of each of the following:

   reign   loose   herd   rode   profit
   rain   lose   heard   rowed   prophet
   check   made   sale   blew   pear
   cheque   maid   sail   blue   pare

4 In what type of book would you find the following information?
   a telephone number
   the meaning of a word
   a list of goods for sale
   the record of a ship's voyage
   a collection of photographs
   the time of a train or bus
   the name of a hotel guest
   a record of personal daily events

1   Suggest a suitable caption for this picture and say why you chose it.
2   Describe how you might feel if you were the girl in the picture.
3   Write a dramatic account of what happened to the girl.

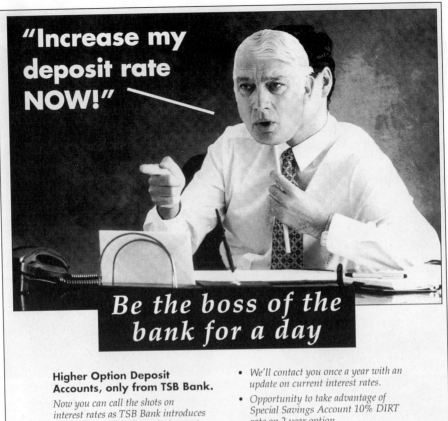

"Increase my deposit rate NOW!"

Be the boss of the bank for a day

Higher Option Deposit Accounts, only from TSB Bank.

Now you can call the shots on interest rates as TSB Bank introduces the Higher Option Deposit Account.

Unlike regular fixed term deposits where your rate is frozen, the unique Higher Option Deposit Account allows you to opt for an even higher rate of interest during the term if rates should rise.

- *Fixed Term - 2 or 3 years.*
- *Guaranteed minimum 6.75% C.A.R.* interest paid on 2 year option.*
- *Guaranteed minimum 7.5% C.A.R.* interest paid on 3 year option.*
- *If interest rates should rise you have one opportunity during the term to opt for an even higher rate.*

- *We'll contact you once a year with an update on current interest rates.*
- *Opportunity to take advantage of Special Savings Account 10% DIRT rate on 2 year option.*
- *Minimum sum invested, £5,000.*

Take the right option now. Talk to TSB Bank about Higher Option Deposit Accounts - and take your opportunity to make a great rate of guaranteed interest even better.

Contact your local branch or Freefone 1800 211 111.

*(Subject to DIRT)

It's what your bank should **TSB** be.
B A N K

1 Explain the significance of the mask in this advertisement.
2 What aspect of this advertisement do you think is the most important? Why?
3 Do you consider this to be an effective advertisement? Give your reasons.
4 Would this advertisement persuade you to open an account at this bank? Explain your answer.

POETRY

➤ Haunted

From out of the wood I watched them shine,
The windows of the haunted house,
Now ruddy as enchanted wine,
Now dark as flittermouse.

There went a thin voice piping airs
Along the grey and crooked walks,
A garden of thistledown and tares,
Bright leaves and giant stalks.

The twilight rain shone at its gates,
Where long-leaved grass in shadow grew;
And back in silence to her mates
A voiceless raven flew.

Lichen and moss the lone stones greened,
Green paths led lightly to its door;
Keen from her lair the spider leaned,
And dusk to darkness wore.

Amidst the sedge a whisper ran,
The West shut down a heavy eye,
And like last tapers, few and wan,
The watch-stars kindled in the sky.

Walter de la Mare

71

1 Why do you think the windows of the house were shining in the first stanza?
2 What evidence is there in the poem to suggest that the house is vacant?
3 What feelings or mood are you left with after reading this poem?
4 The poem is rich in descriptive images. Select some examples and say why you think they are particularly effective.

➤ The Wayfarer

The beauty of the world hath made me sad,
This beauty that will pass;
Sometimes my heart hath shaken with great joy
To see a leaping squirrel in a tree,
Or a red lady-bird upon a stalk
Or little rabbits in a field at evening,
Lit by a slanting sun,
Or some green hill where shadows drifted by,
Some quiet hill where mountainy man hath sown
And soon will reap, near to the gate of Heaven:
Or children with bare feet upon the sands
Of some ebbed sea, or playing on the streets
Of little towns in Connacht,
Things young and happy.
And then my heart hath told me:
These will pass,
Will pass and change, will die and be no more,
Things bright and green, things young and happy;
And I have gone upon my way
Sorrowful.

Padraic Pearse

1 Why do you think the poem is called 'The Wayfarer?'
2 Outline Padraic Pearse's thoughts as they are presented in this poem.
3 What are your favourite lines in the poem? Explain why.
4 Describe your feelings on reading this poem.

➤ Your attention please

The Polar DEW has just warned that
A nuclear rocket strike of
At least one thousand megatons
Has been launched by the enemy
Directly at our major cities.
This announcement will take
Two and a quarter minutes to make,
You therefore have a further
Eight and a quarter minutes
To comply with the shelter
Requirements published in the Civil
Defence Code – section Atomic Attack
A specially shortened Mass
Will be broadcast at the end
Of this announcement -
Protestant and Jewish services
Will begin simultaneously -
Select your wave length immediately
According to instructions
In the Defence Code. Do not
Take well-loved pets (including birds)
Into your shelter – they will consume
Fresh air. Leave the old and bed-
ridden, you can do nothing for them.
Remember to press the sealing
Switch when everyone is in
the shelter. Set the radiation
Aerial; turn on the geiger barometer
Turn off your television now.
Turn off your radio immediately
The Services end. At the same time
Secure explosion plugs in the ears
Of each member of your family. Take
Down your plasma flasks. Give your children
The pills marked one and two
In the CD green container, then put
Them to bed. Do not break
The inside airlock seals until
The radiation All Clear shows
(Watch for the cuckoo in your
perspex panel), or your District
Touring Doctor rings your bell.
If before this, your air becomes
Exhausted or if any of your family

Is critically injured, administer
The capsules marked 'Valley Forge'
(Red Pocket in No. 1 Survival Kit)
For painless death. (Catholics
will have been instructed by their priests
What to do in this eventuality).
This announcement is ending. Our President
Has already given orders for
massive retaliation – it will be
Decisive. Some of us may die.
Remember, statistically
It is not likely to be you.
All flags are flying fully dressed
On Government buildings – the sun is shining.
Death is the least we have to fear.
We are all in the hands of God,
Whatever happens, happens by His Will.
Now go quickly to your shelters.

Peter Porter

uestions

1 Explain briefly the subject matter of this very unusual poem.
2 How did you feel having read this poem?
3 What idea do you think the poet wants to convey in the last three lines of
   the poem?
4 Pick out a number of images or phrases which you like. Explain your
   choice.
5 Suggest an alternative title for this poem and give reasons for your choice.

➤ A sunset poem

Every morning when I wake,
Dear Lord, a little prayer I make,
O please to keep Thy lovely eye
On all poor creatures born to die.

And every evening at sun-down
I ask a blessing on the town,
For whether we last the night or no
I'm sure is always touch-and-go.

We are not wholly bad or good
Who live our lives under Milk Wood.
And Thou, I know, wilt be the first
To see our best side, not our worst.

O let us see another day!
Bless us this night, I pray,
And to the sun we all will bow
And say, good-bye – but just for now!

Dylan Thomas

Questions

1 What do you think is the main theme of this simple poem by Dylan Thomas?

2 How would you describe the poet's attitude to life? Where is it conveyed in the poem?

3 Explain what you think is meant by the lines:
   'We are not wholly bad or good
   Who live our lives under Milk Wood.'

4 Which one of the four stanzas do you prefer? Explain why.

➤ A Case of Murder

They should not have left him there alone,
Alone that is except for the cat.
He was only nine, not old enough
To be left alone in a basement flat,
Alone, that is, except for the cat.
A dog would have been a different thing.
A big gruff dog with slashing jaws,
But a cat with round eyes mad as gold,
Plump as a cushion with tucked-in paws –
Better have left him with a fair-sized rat!
But what they did was leave him with a cat.
He hated that cat; he watched it sit,
A buzzing machine of soft black stuff,
He sat and watched and he hated it,
Smug in its fur, hot blood in a muff,
And its mad gold stare and the way it sat
Crooning dark warmth: he loathed all that.
So he took Daddy's stick and he hit the cat.
Then quick as a sudden crack in glass
It hissed, black flash, to a hiding place
In the dust and dark beneath the couch,
And he followed the grin on his new-made face,
A wide-eyed, frightened snarl of a grin,
And he took the stick and he thrust it in,
Hard and quick in the furry dark.
The black fur squealed and he felt his skin
Prickle with sparks of dry delight.
Then the cat again came into sight,
Shot for the door that wasn't quite shut,
But the boy, quick too, slammed fast the door:
The cat, half-through, was cracked like a nut
And the soft black thud was dumped on the floor.
Then the boy was suddenly terrified
And he bit his knuckles and cried and cried;
But he had to do something with the dead thing there.
His eyes squeezed beads of salty prayer
But the wound of fear gaped wide and raw;
He dared not touch the thing with his hands
So he fetched a spade and shovelled it
And dumped the load of heavy fur
In the spidery cupboard under the stair
Where it's been for years, and though it died
It's grown in that cupboard and its hot low purr

Grows slowly louder year by year:
There'll not be a corner for the boy to hide
When the cupboard swells and all sides split
And the huge black cat pads out of it.

Vernon Scannell

 uestions

1   Suggest some reasons why the young boy hated the cat.
2   From the evidence of the poem what type of person do you imagine the boy
    to be?
3   How would you describe the atmosphere in the poem? How does the poet
    manage to create this atmosphere?
4   Explain briefly what images the poet meant to convey in the following
    lines:
    (a) 'Plump as a cushion with tucked-in paws'
    (b) 'Prickle with sparks of dry delight'
    (c) 'In the spidery cupboard under the stair'
5   What do you think the poet meant in the last three lines of the poem?

➤ In Memory of My Mother

I do not think of you lying in the wet clay
Of a Monaghan graveyard: I see
You walking down a lane among the poplars
On your way to the station, or happily

Going to second Mass on a summer Sunday
You meet me and you say:
'Don't forget to see about the cattle –'
Among your earthiest words the angels stray.

And I think of you walking along a headland
Of green oats in June,
So full of repose, so rich with life –
And I see us meeting at the end of a town
On a fair day by accident, after
The bargains are all made and we can walk
Together through the shops and stalls and markets
Free in the oriental streets of thought.

O you are not lying in the wet clay,
For it is a harvest evening now and we
Are piling up the ricks against the moonlight
and you smile up at us – eternally.

Patrick Kavanagh

Questions

1   The poet seems to have been very close to his mother. What evidence is there in the poem to suggest this?
2   From the evidence of the poem what type of person do you think the poet's mother was? Explain your answer.
3   Explain briefly what you think the poet meant by the following lines:
    (a) 'Among your earthiest words the angels stray'
    (b) 'Free in the oriental streets of thought'
4   The ordinary happenings of rural life in Ireland are seen by the poet in a romantic light. How does Kavanagh do this and for what purpose?
5   The poet uses a system of run-on lines in the poem. What effect has this on the poem?
6   How would you describe the tone of this poem? Explain your answer.

➤ London Spring 1941

If I could paint I'd show you
Something I saw to-day;
A house bombed, blasted sideways,
A roof blown clean away;
A bath perched near a chasm;
A waste of broken floors,
The staircase turned to matchwood
And twisted, tortured doors.
While in the neighbour's garden,
With slender fence and tree
Dividing all its modest length
From dark catastrophe,
A little Moses cradle
Was placed upon the ground
And in it slept a baby
So pink and sweet and round,
With no one there to mind it,
To fuss or fear, not one!
But all the jolly crocuses
Wide open to the sun.

Eiluned Lewis

Questions

1 Why do you think the poet would prefer to paint a picture of the scene rather than describe it in words?
2 This is a poem of contrasts. In what ways is this statement true?
3 Suggest an alternative title for the poem and give reasons for your choice.
4 How would you describe the mood of the poem? Explain your answer.
5 Explain what you think the poet means by the following lines:
  (a) 'A bath perched near a chasm;
       A waste of broken floors.'
  (b) 'Dividing all its modest length
       From dark catastrophe.'

UNIT 7

➤ His Majesty O'Connor

Dennis O'Connor wiped the sweat off his forehead and put down his pen. The day had been hot, and the stones of the prison seemed to have shut all the heat inside his cell. The light from the iron-barred window above his head was fading. The square of sky changed from blue to pearl colour as he looked at it.

Dennis rubbed his tired eyes and lay down on the heap of rushes that softened the hardness of the stone floor a little. His head ached from writing all day and from the stuffiness of his cell. He looked very thin as he lay there. His face in the fading light was almost the colour of the paper on which he had been writing.

A key grated in the lock of his door, and the jailer's voice roared 'Come into the court, King O'Connor. The banquet is ready for your Majesty.'

The prisoners ate at a rough table in the courtyard. Dennis sat down on a bench beside a huge negro. The banquet consisted of wooden bowls full of a sour-smelling, greasy stew and hunks of soggy grey bread.

The jailer said, 'Your Majesty is not eating anything. You don't seem to like our roast peacock.'

Dennis did not like being called 'Your Majesty'. It had never seemed very funny, and he had been tired of the joke for a long time. He had lost his temper once and said to the jailer that his – Dennis's – ancestors had been kings in Connaught when the jailer's grandfathers were already jailers. It was a foolish speech, and he had paid for it in many ways. Being laughed at was only one of them, and far from the worst. Being forced to eat the jail-food was bad. It was not safe to leave anything in his bowl. It would only be served to him the next day, tasting worse than ever. And if he refused then, the jailer might take away his pen and papers. Dennis dreaded that worse than being kept in his cell all day, or being lashed with a whip, an exercise the jailer enjoyed.

He dipped his piece of bread into the stew and tried to eat it. When the jailer turned his head away, Dennis slid his bowl along to the negro and whispered, 'Eat it, Fernan, I can't.'

The negro, Fernan Martinez, had been polishing his bowl with the crust of his bread. He pushed the empty bowl to Dennis and began on the full one. He dipped his huge black fingers into the bowl, crammed the meat and onions into his mouth, then tipped his woolly head back and poured the liquid down his throat. He finished by sopping up the last of the juice with Dennis's bread. He chewed loudly, showing enormous white teeth and turning every now and then to smile at Dennis.

Louise Andrews Kent

 uestions

1   How is Dennis described in the second paragraph?
2   Do you think the word 'banquet' is a good description of the food? Why?
3   How did Dennis feel about the jailer?
4   Give two reasons to explain why the jailer thought that he was being funny when he called the meal 'roast peacock'.
5   Is there anything in the passage to prove that Dennis was fond of writing even though it tired him?
6   Explain why Fernan is described as having a 'woolly' head.
7   This extract is written from the point of view of the prisoner. Write two paragraphs from the jailer's point of view.

POETRY

➤ An introduction to dogs

The dog is man's best friend.
He has a tail on one end.
Up in front he has teeth.
And four legs underneath.

Dogs like to bark.
They like it best after dark.
They not only frighten prowlers away
But also hold the sandman at bay.

A dog that is indoors
To be let out implores.
You let him out and what then?
He wants back in again.

Dogs display reluctance and wrath
If you try to give them a bath.
They bury bones in hideaways
And half the time they trot sideaways.

They cheer up people who are frowning,
And rescue people who are drowning,
They also track mud on beds,
And chew people's clothes to shreds.

Dogs in the country have fun.
They run and run and run.
But in the city this species
Is dragged around on leashes.

Dogs are upright as a steeple
And much more loyal than people.

                                    Ogden Nash

Questions

1   'The dog is man's best friend'. Show from the poem that this statement
    might be true.
2   Why can it be said that dogs would prefer the country to the town?
3   Pick out some words or phrases from this poem which you like and say why
    you chose them.
4   Are the last two lines in the poem an appropriate ending? Give your
    reasons.

Which drill would you prefer your kids get used to?

NEW NEW NEW NEW NEW NEW NEW NEW NEW NEW NEW NEW NEW NEW NEW NEW NEW NEW NEW NEW

GREAT TASTE

SB

macleans
JUNIOR
MOUTH
GUARD

FIGHTS PLAQUE
STRENGTHENS TEETH
HELPS PREVENT TOOTH DECAY

By the time they're twelve, 53% of children suffer from some form of tooth decay. And where tooth decay strikes, the drill soon follows.

That's something nobody relishes, least of all a dentist. So what exactly can you do to help?

Well, obviously make sure your kids have regular check-ups. And, of course, insist they brush after meals.

But you should also get them into the habit of using Macleans Junior Mouth Guard at least twice a day.

This is a mouthwash that has been specially formulated to provide young teeth with unbeatable protection. To that end, it contains a bacterial agent to attack plaque, plus fluoride to strengthen the teeth.

And because it's a liquid, it gets everywhere in the mouth, even those places a kid's toothbrush can't.

There's something else in our favour: kids love its great taste. It's one drill they don't mind getting used to.

Macleans where a kid's toothbrush can't.

1   Give reasons why you think this is an effective advertisement.
2   The props are an important feature of the advertisement. Explain why this is true.
3   Describe how the advertisement plays on words to convey its message.

1   You have just returned from a rock concert by a world famous group. Write a **letter** to a friend, who was unable to attend, in which you describe the occasion. Try to convey to him/her a sense of the atmosphere at the concert.

2   Write a **story** called *The Clue* beginning:
    The moon threw flickering shadows across our path as we crept towards the silent house....
    and ending with:
    We had solved the mystery of the haunted house.

3   Write a **composition** on one of the following titles:
    (a) Cruelty to animals   (c) Christmas in our house
    (b) Why I like/hate babysitting   (d) Schools of the future

GRAMMAR

1   The correct word in each of the following spaces is either *there* or *their*. Write out the sentences in your copy and fill in the spaces.
    When school was over, all the boys and girls put ____ books in ____ schoolbags and raced into the playground. Many parents were ____ waiting for them, but ____ were some children who had to find ____ own way home.

2   Correct one error in each of the following:
    (a) The girl is wore out from lack of sleep.
    (b) She is to excited to sit down.
    (c) Checks are issued by the banks.

3   Spelling test
committee	whiskey	celery	casualty	interval
medicine	horizon	atmosphere	cupboard	scholar
ceiling	surgeon	mechanic	woollen	stomach
salmon	punctual	introduce	poison	curious

4   Explain each of the following expressions by using them properly in a sentence:
    the lion's share   give the cold shoulder
    on the pig's back   turn over a new leaf
    long in the tooth   draw the line
    break the ice   face the music
    put your best foot forward   sling mud

5   Punctuate the following passage:
    youre in serious trouble now whispered aoife thats mrs burkes window youve broken and shell be teaching you next year at st patricks college

UNIT 8

READING

➤ A night alarm

In the dark hour before the dawn, two nights later, Marcus was roused out of his sleep by the Duty Centurion. A pilot lamp always burned in his sleeping-cell against just such an emergency, and he was fully awake on the instant.

'What is it, Centurion?'

'The sentries on the south rampart report sounds of movement between us and the town, sir'.

Marcus was out of bed and had swung his heavy military cloak over his sleeping-tunic. 'You have been up yourself?'

The Centurion stood aside for him to pass out into the darkness. 'I have, sir', he said with grim patience.

'Anything to be seen?'

'No, sir, but there is something stirring down there, for all that.'

Quickly they crossed the main street of the fort, and turned down beside a row of silent workshops. They were mounting the steps to the rampart walk. The shape of a sentry's helmet rose dark against the lesser darkness above the breastwork, and there was a rustle and thud as he grounded his pilum in salute.

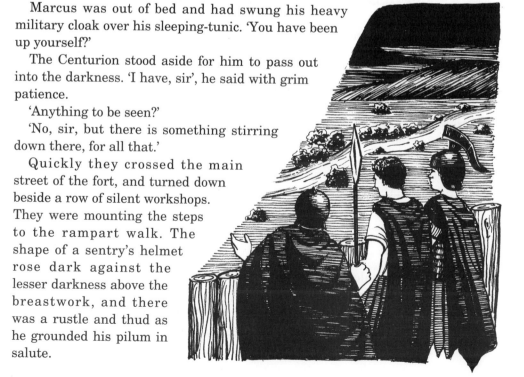

Marcus went to the breast-high parapet. The sky had clouded over so that not a star was to be seen, and all below was a formless blackness with nothing visible save the faint pallor of the river looping through it. Not a breath of air stirred in the stillness, and Marcus listening, heard no sound in all the world save the whisper of the blood in his own ears, far fainter than the sea in the conch-shell.

He waited, breath in check; then from somewhere below came the kee-wick, kee-wick, kee-wick, kee-wick of a hunting owl, and a moment later a faint and formless sound of movement that was gone almost before he could be sure that he had not imagined it. He felt the Duty Centurion grow tense as a strung bow beside him. The moments crawled by, the silence became a physical pressure on his eardrums. Then the sounds came again, and with the sounds, blurred forms moved suddenly on the darkness of the open turf below the ramparts.

Marcus could almost hear the twang of breaking tension. The sentry swore softly under his breath, and the Centurion laughed.

'Somebody will be spending a busy day looking for his strayed cattle!'

Rosemary Sutcliff *The Eagle of the Ninth*

uestions

1 Why was Marcus roused from his sleep?
2 Why were Marcus and the Centurion alarmed by the report of the sentries?
3 What did the two men pass on their way to the rampart walk?
4 What were the blurred forms that moved below the ramparts?
5 What was a Centurion?
6 How do you know that the sentry and the Centurion are relieved by what is discovered?
7 Show that Marcus is superior in rank to the Centurion by mentioning two details from the extract.
8 Why do you think the author chose to use the following words:
   ● grim
   ● formless
   ● crawled
   ● twang
9 Write a short dialogue between Marcus and the Centurion as they walked towards the ramparts.

WHAT I HAVE READ

- Choose a **play** that you have read.
- Give a brief account of the story of the play as you saw it.
- What character was most alive to you? Give your reasons.

PERSONAL AND FUNCTIONAL WRITING

1   You are living in a rented house which is in very bad repair. Write a **letter** of complaint to the landlord, asking for immediate action.

2   You have lost a valuable bicycle which you borrowed from a friend. You haven't the courage to face her/him so you decide to write a **note** instead. Explain the circumstances of the loss and say that you will replace the bicycle.

3   Write a **composition** on one of the following titles.
    (a) Lost in the jungle   (c) My favourite actor or singer
    (b) Springtime in Ireland   (d) Jobs I hate doing

GRAMMAR

1   Insert the correct word in each of the following sentences:
    The climber was careful (lest, except) he should fall.
    Your attitude is different (of, to, from) mine.
    The lion went in pursuit (to, of) the deer.
    To (who, whom) does he wish to speak?
    Mary divided the orange (between, among) her two sisters.
    The children could neither read (or, nor) write.

2   Correct one error in each of the following:
    (a) This book was wrote by a famous author.
    (b) The winning crew were congratulated by the Mayor.
    (c) Each of the players have a racquet.

3   Punctuate the following passage:
    george p crowley joined the firm of brennan and doyle as an office boy just before the outbreak of world war two today he is managing director the company has expanded greatly under his guidance it has offices in paris rome london and geneva

4   Write down the opposites of the following words by adding a prefix:
    agree   important   legal   visible   proper
    sense   loyal   noble   pleasant   human

1 Suggest a suitable title for the picture and give reasons for your choice.
2 How would you describe the expression on the old man's face?
3 From the evidence of the picture, what type of person do you imagine the old man to be?
4 Imagine that you are the old man in the picture. Write an interesting account of your life.

It may be small but it's all we've got.

It seems obvious, but the way that some people treat the world, you would think there is somewhere else to go once the earth's resources have been exhausted.

You know there isn't. Our small planet is being ravaged and its limited resources are fast disappearing.

This is why Greenpeace is trying to protect our fragile planet.

By applying international direct action with scientific research and political pressure, Greenpeace has had many notable successes.

The atmospheric testing of Nuclear weapons by the French in the Pacific has been stopped.

Commercial whaling is in the process of being stopped.

Dumping of radioactive waste in the ocean has been stopped.

The large scale commercial slaughter of baby harp seals in Canada has been stopped.

Incineration at sea of dangerous toxic chemicals has been stopped.

But at Greenpeace, we don't want to stop everything. What we have started is a general raising of the awareness of the environment across the globe. However, there is still a long way to go.

Deforestation and the depletion of the ozone layer are just two major problems we are aiming to overcome; there are countless others.

To carry on the work we urgently need your help. Greenpeace is a non-profit organisation supported by memberships and donations.

To find out how you can help, fill out the Greenpeace coupon and mail it today.

1 Explain in your own words what the headline of this advertisement means.
2 Write a paragraph summarising the work of Greenpeace.
3 Why do you think the organisation is called Greenpeace?
4 In what ways can people in Ireland support the work of organisations like Greenpeace?

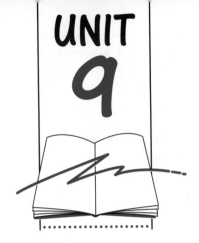

UNIT 9

READING

➤ Walkabout

The three children stood looking at each other in the middle of the Australian desert. Motionless as the outcrops of granite they stared, and stared, and stared. Between them the distance was less than the spread of an outstretched arm, but more than a hundred thousand years.

Brother and sister were products of the highest strata of humanity's evolution. In them the primitive had long ago been swept aside, been submerged by mechanisation, been swamped by scientific development, been nullified by the standardised pattern of the white man's way of life. They had climbed a long way up the ladder of progress; they had climbed so far, in fact, that they had forgotten how their climb had started. Coddled in babyhood, psycho-analysed in childhood, nourished on predigested patent foods, provided with continuous push-button entertainment, the basic realities of life were something they'd never had to face.

It was very different with the Aboriginal. He knew what reality was. He led a way of life that was already old when Tut-ankh-amen started to build his tomb; a way of life that had been tried and proved before the white man's continents were even lifted out of the sea. Among the secret water-holes of the Australian desert his people had lived and died, unchanged and unchanging, for twenty thousand years. Their lives were unbelievably simple. They had no homes, no crops, no clothes, no possessions. The few things they had, they shared: food and wives; children and laughter; tears and hunger and thirst. They walked from one water-hole to the next; they exhausted one supply of food, then moved on to another. Their lives were utterly uncomplicated because they were devoted to one purpose, dedicated in their entirety to the waging of one battle: the battle with death. Death was their ever-present enemy. He sought them out from every dried-up salt pan, from the flames of every bush fire. He was never far away. Keeping him at bay was the Aboriginals' full-time job: the job they'd been doing for twenty thousand years: the job they were good at.

The desert sun streamed down. The children stared and stared. Mary had decided not to move. To move would be a sign of weakness. She remembered being told about the man who'd come face to face with a lion, and had stared it out, had caused it to slink discomfited away. That was what she'd do to the black boy; she'd stare at him until he felt the shame of his nakedness and slunk away. She thrust out her chin, and glared.

Peter had decided to take his cue from his sister. Clutching her hand he stood waiting: waiting for something to happen.

The Aboriginal was in no hurry. Time had little value to him. His next meal – the rock wallaby – was assured. Water was near. Tomorrow was also a day. For the moment he was content to examine these strange creatures at his leisure. Their clumsy, lumbering movements intrigued him; their lack of weapons indicated their harmlessness. His eyes moved slowly, methodically from one to another: examining them from head to foot. They were the first white people a member of his tribe had ever seen.

Mary, beginning to resent this scrutiny, intensified her glare. But the bush boy seemed in no way perturbed: his appraisal went methodically on.

After a while Peter started to fidget. The delay was fraying his nerves. He wished someone would do something: wished something would happen. Then, quite involuntarily, he himself started a new train of events. His head began to waggle: his nose tilted skywards; he spluttered and choked; he tried to hold his breath; but all in vain. It had to come. He sneezed.

It was a mighty sneeze for such a little fellow: the release of a series of explosions, all the more violent for having been dammed back. To his sister the sneeze was a calamity. She had just intensified her stare to the point – she felt sure – of irresistibility; when the spell was shattered. The bush boy's attention shifted from her to Peter.

Frustration warped her sense of justice. She condemned her brother out of court; was turning on him angrily, when a second sneeze, even mightier than the first, shattered the silence of the bush.

Mary raised here eyes to heaven: invoking the gods as witnesses to her despair. But the vehemence of the second sneeze was still tumbling leaves from the humble-bushes, when a new sound made her whirl around. A gust of laughter: melodious laughter; low at first, then becoming louder: unrestrained: disproportionate: uncontrolled.

She looked at the bush boy in amazement. He was doubled up with belly-shaking spasms of mirth.

Peter's incongruous, out-of-proportion sneeze had touched off one of his peoples' most highly developed traits: a sense of the ridiculous; a sense so keenly felt as to be almost beyond control. The bush boy laughed with complete abandon. He flung himself to the ground. He rolled head-over-heels in unrestrained delight.

His mirth was infectious. It woke in Peter an instant response: a like appreciation of the ludicrous. The guilt that the little boy had started to feel, melted away. At first apologetically, then whole-heartedly, he too started to laugh.

The barrier of twenty thousand years vanished in the twinkling of an eye. The boy's laughter echoed back from the granite rocks. They started to strike comic postures, each striving to outdo the other in their grotesque abandon.

Mary watched them. She would have dearly loved to join in. A year ago – in her tom-boy days – she would have. But not now. She was too sensible: too grown-up. Yet not grown-up enough to be free of an instinctive longing to share in the fun: to throw convention to the winds and join the capering jamboree. This longing she repressed. She stood aloof: disapproving. At last she went up to Peter and took his hand.

'That's enough, Peter,' she said.

The skylarking subsided. For a moment there was silence, then the bush boy spoke.

'*Worumgala?* (Where do you come from?) His voice was lilting as his laughter.

Mary and Peter looked at each other blankly.

The bush boy tried again.

'*Worum mwa?* (Where are you going?)

It was Peter, not Mary, who floundered into the field of conversation. 'We dun'no what you're talking about, darkie. But we're lost, see. We want to go to Adelaide. That's where Uncle Keith lives. Which way do we go?'

James Vance Marshall

Questions

1 Why did Mary decide not to move?
2 The young Aboriginal boy was in no hurry. Explain why this was so.
3 Why was Mary annoyed with Peter?
4 Why do you think the Aboriginal boy started to laugh when Peter sneezed?
5 Explain in your own words the following sentence taken from the extract:
   'Between them the distance was less than the spread of an outstretched arm, but more than a hundred thousand years'
6 From the evidence of the extract, what type of person do you imagine Mary to be?
7 The extract contains a number of very difficult words. Look up each of the following in your dictionary and use each one in a sentence of your own.
   perturbed, scrutiny, involuntarily, mirth, infectious, ludicrous, instinctive, aloof.
8 The story is set in the Australian outback. What, in your opinion, would be the greatest problems for a city boy or girl lost in the Australian bush?
9 The extract leaves you guessing as to what happened next. Write your own conclusion to the story.

POETRY

> ## The sculptor

I took a piece of plastic clay
And idly fashioned it, one day,
And as my fingers pressed it, still
It moved and yielded to my will.

I came again, when days were passed,
That bit of clay was hard at last,
The form I gave it, still it bore,
And I could change that form no more.

Then I took a piece of living clay
And gently formed it, day by day,
And molded with my power and art,
A young child's soft and yielding heart.

I came again when years were gone,
It was a man I looked upon,
He still that early impress bore,
And I could change it, nevermore.

Author Unknown

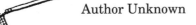

Questions

1 Why was it possible to mold the clay into different shapes?
2 This poem can be said to have two parts. Explain why this is so.
3 Explain what you think is meant by the line
   'And gently formed it, day by day,'
4 What lesson is to be found in the last two lines of the poem?
5 What impression does this poem make on you?

1   Suggest a suitable title for this picture and give reasons for your choice.
2   How would you describe the expression on the players face?
3   What do you think were the player's thoughts at that particular moment?
4   Write a dramatic account of the final moments of a game of tennis.

IT'S FLAMING GREAT.

IT'S ELECTRIC!

People used to say there's nothing like a real fire, but now there is - Optiflame.

Optiflame has all the beauty and warmth of a real fire without the inconvenience or the cost. To fill your hearth with the effect of an open fire, simply plug in and switch on. There's no dirty coals, troublesome lighting or messy cleaning, just clean warm comfort.

And there's no installation costs because you just plug in. Optiflame is flexible and can be moved from room to room with ease.

Optiflame fires have built-in-energy saving features. You set the temperature you want; Optiflame automatically switches on and off to keep the room temperature constant.

With a choice of styles and starting at only £249, there's an Optiflame to suit your home.

Optiflame ®™
by Dimplex

AVAILABLE FROM ELECTRICAL RETAILERS AND ESB SHOPS NATIONWIDE

1 What is the connection between the headline and the photograph?
2 Props are chosen very carefully when an advertiser is trying to create a mood. Explain the choice of props used here. What mood is created by the props which are used in this advertisement?
3 Comment on the language used by the advertiser in this advertisement.
4 Could this advertisement work without the use of any written information? What is your opinion of advertisements which do not include a picture?

1   You have an article for sale. It might be a bicycle, a radio, or some small item of sports gear. Write out an **advertisement,** offering the article for sale, describing it in the most attractive way you can.

2   Write a **newspaper report** of the hardships caused by a severe snowstorm.

3   Write a **composition** on one of the following titles:
    (a) My favourite television programmes
    (b) Moving to a new school
    (c) The day the spaceship landed
    (d) A family outing I would like to forget

GRAMMAR

1   Complete the following expressions, in your copy, by filling in the missing words:

as blind as _____	as quiet as _____
as slow as _____	as strong as _____
as sober as _____	as wise as _____
as cunning as _____	as white as _____
as proud as _____	as obstinate as _____

Use each expression in a suitable sentence.

2   Correct one error in each of the following:
    (a) He gave me a lend of his car.
    (b) The younger of the three boys was only six.
    (c) She choose the best dress in the boutique.

3   Write out the opposites of the following words:

exit	laugh	thick	stop
enemy	ancient	beginning	private
sober	best	tight	noisy
wide	outside	last	tame

4. Fill the gaps.
    Write the following in your copy, filling in the missing words.
    The first pen was probably a piece _____ reed, or rush stem. Since then, we have had pens made _____ quills, metal nibs, and ball points. Modern _____ now have fibre tips, rather _____ the first pens which were invented. _____ year, over a hundred million pens are _____. They now come in bright _____, not just blue or black.
       You can _____ a fibre tip pen for any purpose, for writing _____ drawing. _____ pens have fine lines, whereas drawing pens make _____ lines.

In the middle of a fibre _____ pen is a long piece of material soaked in _____. As ink is rubbed off the tip, more is _____ up from the middle to take _____ place. Some pens will _____ for 500 feet before being used up. Others _____ write for 2,000 feet before running _____.

If you leave off the _____ of your pen, you will lose at _____ one fifth of the ink in a month. With some pens _____ can lose three quarters of the ink by _____ off the pen top.

Some pens have screw _____, others just push on. If the top _____ off in your pocket, you _____ have a nasty mess.

All fibre tip pens have tips _____ get broader as you write, but _____ pens have tips which broaden _____ easily than others. This can be a nuisance _____ you choose a pen that writes _____ a fine line, but which spreads quickly so that you can _____ make a fine line any _____.

4 If you solve this puzzle correctly, the first column down will make two words that tell you whose digging tool it is. Choose your words from this list:

bandage   voyage   stage   savage   courage   advantage
postage   manage   engage   average   damage   sabotage

1 A raised platform on which you act

2 Medium

3 To control

4 Not civilised; fierce

5 Deliberate damage to the enemy's property

6 The charge for sending letters by post

7 To be 'one-up' on somebody

8 To cause harm or injury

9 To take on or employ

READING

➤ The fight

I was standing at the end of the lower playground and annoying Mr Samuels, who lived in the house just below the high railings. Mr Samuels complained once a week that boys from the school threw apples and stones and balls through his bedroom window. He sat in a deck chair in a small square of trim garden and tried to read the newspaper. I was only a few yards from him. I was staring him out. He pretended not to notice me, but I knew he knew I was standing there rudely and quietly. Every now and then he peeped at me from behind his newspaper, saw me still and serious and alone, with my eyes on his. As soon as he lost his temper I was going to go home. Already I was late for dinner. I had almost beaten him, the newspaper was trembling, he was breathing heavily, when a strange boy, whom I had not heard approach, pushed me down the bank.

   I threw a stone at his face. He took off his spectacles, put them in his coat pocket, took off his coat, hung it neatly on the railings, and attacked. Turning round as we wrestled on the top of the bank, I saw that Mr Samuels had folded his newspaper on the deck chair and was standing up to watch us. It was a mistake to turn round. The strange boy rabbit-punched me twice. Mr Samuels hopped with excitement as I fell against the railings. I was down in the dust, hot and scratched and biting, then up and dancing. and I butted the boy in the belly and we tumbled in a heap. I saw through a closing eye that his nose was bleeding. I hit his nose. He tore at my collar and spun me round by the hair.

   'Come on! come on!' I heard Mr Samuels cry.

   We both turned towards him. He was shaking his fists and dodging about in the garden. He stopped then, and coughed, and set his panama straight, and avoided our eyes, and turned his back and walked slowly to the deck chair.

   We both threw gravel at him.

   'I'll give him 'Come on!' the boy said, as we ran along the playground away from the shouts of Mr Samuels and down the steps on to the hill.

We walked home together. I admired his bloody nose. He said that my eye was like a poached egg, only black.

'I've never seen such a lot of blood,' I said.

He said I had the best black eye in Wales, perhaps it was the best black eye in Europe; he bet Tunney never had a black eye like that.

'And there's blood all over your shirt.'

'Sometimes I bleed in dollops,' he said.

On Walter's Road we passed a group of high school girls and I cocked my cap and hoped my eye was as big as a bluebag and he walked with his coat flung open to show the bloodstains.

I was a hooligan all during dinner, and a bully, and as bad as a boy from the Sandbanks, and I should have more respect, and I sat silently, like Tunney, over the sago pudding. That afternoon I went to school with an eye-shade on. If I had had a black silk sling I would have been as gay and desperate as the wounded captain in the book that my sister used to read, and that I read under the bed-clothes at night, secretly with a flash-lamp.

Dylan Thomas *Portrait of the Artist as a young dog*

Questions

1   What was the boy's aim in staring at Mr Samuels and what proof is there that he was achieving his purpose?
2   Why do you think, did Dylan turn round to look at Mr Samuels in the middle of the fight?
3   Why did Mr Samuels behave as he did when the two boys turned towards him?

4 What made the boys suddenly become friends?
5 Explain why the boys behaved as they did when they passed the girls.
6 From the evidence of the extract, what type of person do you imagine Mr Samuels to be?
7 What do you think Dylan Thomas means when he says that he was 'a hooligan all during dinner'?
8 Gene Tunney was a famous boxer. Why are the references to him particularly appropriate in this extract?
9 Write a brief dialogue between the two boys as they walked home after the fight.

PERSONAL AND FUNCTIONAL WRITING

1 Write a suitable **reply** to one of the following job advertisements.

TRAINEE MANAGER

Required for Dublin Southside Quark Store. Applicants must be over 20 years of age. Must be experienced in all aspects of the supermarket business. The successful applicant will be self motivated, able to work as a team member and have ideas to benefit a fast growing business. Apply in writing with full c.v. and references to

Box NO: P.O. 2500X

HAIRSTYLISTS
(Qualified)

ANDREW PARK
Dublin/Carlow/Waterford

Opportunities exist to join busy, first class hairstyling teams at Andrew Park Salons throughout Dublin, Carlow and Waterford. If you are talented, ambitious and want to develop your hairdressing skills with further training,
Apply in writing to Andrew Park Salons, The Glen, Ballybofey.

HOTEL CONSTANCE DUBLIN
Requires an
Assistant Restaurant Manager

for busy operation. The ideal candidate should have strong leadership, organisational and guest relations skills along with a minimum of 3 years experience in a hotel of similar standing.
Applications, in writing only, enclosing a full C.V. to:

**Ms. Irene Fitzhugh,
Personnel Department,
Hotel Constance Dublin,
Blakefield Terrace, Dublin 2.**

2   Write a **short story** beginning with the words:
    The clatter of the letterbox told me that the school report had arrived.

3   Write a **composition** on one of the following titles.
    (a) A haunted house
    (b) If I won the Lotto
    (c) An exciting football match
    (d) Getting up on a winter's morning

GRAMMAR

1   Punctuate the following passage:
    how many boys are there in this class twenty three i can see only twenty
    two john ryan is missing today he had to go to dublin with his father he
    didnt tell me he was going he had to go suddenly his father has an urgent
    appointment

2   The following words have more than one meaning. Write sentences giving
    as many meanings as you can for each word.

    cross   crook   cricket   jam   lead
    mine   park   permit   pick   plant

3   Suggest a suitable word for the spaces below:
    Boy is to girl as _____ is to woman.
    Soldier is to ____ as sailor is to navy.
    Sheep is to mutton as pig is to _____.
    Food is to hungry as _____ is to thirsty.
    Wing is to _____ as fin is to fish.
    Flock is to sheep as _____ is to cattle.
    Whisper is to shout as walk is to _____.
    Steamer is to pier as train is to _____.

4   Correct one error in each of the following:
    (a) The committee have decided to resign.
    (b) Drink has a bad effect on some people.
    (c) Paul could not run no faster.

5   Spelling test

generous	transparent	principal	ignorant	diamond
burglar	prominent	reduction	pause	threaten
exception	drought	instrument	glorious	religion
behaviour	staggered	abundant	colourful	barrel

1 Suggest an appropriate title for this picture and say why you chose it.
2 How does this picture make you feel?
3 Write a short story based on this picture.
4 Write an accurate and objective description of what you see in this picture.

"LOCAL"...

....RADIO....

"HERE, THERE AND **EVERYWHERE"** ... that's the good news about local radio stations in Ireland - their listeners are spread across the country, in every village, town and city. The fact is that 56%* of those who listen to radio, listen to local radio. It's a fact worth noting, if you want to get your message across!

CONTACT THE SALES AGENTS FOR IRS

61 LOWER BAGGOT STREET DUBLIN 2. TEL 01 6616575 FAX 01 6763191

1   At whom is this particular advertisement targeted? Explain your answer.
2   Comment on the effectiveness of the written part (the copy) of the advertisement.
3   Can you imagine what the two people are discussing? Write a short dialogue.
4   Which type of radio do you prefer, local or national? Explain your reasons.

UNIT
11

READING

➤ Slavery

Morning came to the slave quarters of Master Hensen's plantation before there was light in the heavy, black sky. It was four o'clock and Master Hensen's old ram horn bellowed and tooted until nobody slept. Frying sowbelly smells from the cabin cooking fires helped wake the children. Julilly reached for the hoecake and a tin cup of buttermilk that Mammy Sally poured. From the barnyard the roosters crowed sharp and clear.

As on every other morning, Julilly smoothed down her crinkly hair and twisted it tight in a knot at the back of her head. But Mammy Sally, who always wore a clean, white head-bag neatly tied, this morning put on a black one in its place. There was no laughter in her full, strong voice as she called to one slave and then another who passed by their door. A worried frown stitched lines across her forehead.

'Child,' she said to Julilly in a yearning, mournful way, 'there's trouble ahead for us nigger folk today.'

Her lips pinched firm and her eyes flamed with angry courage, but her voice stayed quiet. She gathered Julilly's hands into the strength of her long, black, calloused fingers.

'Lord help us,' she said. 'The field hands are gonna be sold today. You are one of them June Lilly. You and I could be pulled apart.'

Julilly couldn't understand. Mammy Sally couldn't let this happen.

Mammy shook Julilly into listening. 'If we are sold apart, June Lilly, and the Lord forbid, don't forget that freedom land I told you about. You and I are strong. We'll get there with the guidance of that star, and the good Lord's help.'

A jay-bird voice screeched suddenly outside their door.

'You field-hand niggers. Line yourselves up along this path and don't you loiter.' The sound of a zinging whip cut the air. 'Some of you ain't gonna chop no cotton today.'

Mammy Sally held Julilly close as they walked outside and joined the field-hand line. The man with the jay-bird voice strode back and forth in front of them. He was a big man with a short, thick neck. His cheeks puffed and juggled as he walked. Julilly noticed that his fingers puffed, too, over the whip that he flicked in his hand. He had a toothpick in his mouth that stuck between two yellow teeth. Julilly didn't like his oily skin. His faded brown hair was tangled and dirty, his baggy pants were streaked with drippings and his little eyes were green and sly.

He strode towards Lilly Brown, a shy young mother barely sixteen. She clutched her two-year-old Willie in her arms.

The fat man paused briefly beside her. His tiny eyes narrowed and he rubbed his oily hand down Willie's bare back.

'This is a fat, strong nigger baby,' he called to a younger white man behind him. 'Put him in the wagon.'

Willie was ripped from his mother's arms without a comment.

Lilly screamed and fell to the ground.

Julilly started to run towards her, but the firm hand of Mammy Sally grasped her shoulder.

The fat man was stopping in front of them, clamping the toothpick hard between his lips. He stuck a fat finger into her mouth and squinted at her teeth. Satisfied, he pushed back her eyelids.

'Looking at me like Old John does his horse,' Julilly thought and flamed with anger.

'This one will do,' the big man called towards the young man who had just dumped Willie in the cart. 'She's strong and healthy and still growin'. Get over there, girl, and get into that cart.' He strode off down the line.

Julilly didn't move. She looked at Mammy, and for the first time in her life saw fear in Mammy Sally's eyes.

'Do like he say, child,' Mammy's voice hurt and choked. 'You got to mind that man in order to save your life. Don't forget that place I told you about.'

The fat man looked back and screeched,

'Get in that wagon, girl or I'll use this whip and teach you how to jump.'

There was moaning now and crying up and down the line of slaves. The big slave trader didn't care or hear. He lashed his whip in the air, pulling children from their mothers and fathers, sending them to the cart.

Julilly moved towards the long, wooden cart. Her feet pulled her there somehow and she climbed inside. She looked for Mammy Sally, but Mammy was already being pushed with the older slaves far down beyond the tool shed.

Julilly strained to find Mammy's black head-bag. It was gone. Mammy Sally had disappeared!

A red sun boiled up into the sky, making patches of heat wherever it struck the uncovered earth. Julilly sat still and numb in the unshaded wagon. Little Willie Brown whimpered beside her. She wanted to comfort him, but she couldn't lift her hand. She found it hard to swallow and wondered if she could make a sound if she tried to speak.

Other children began climbing into the wagon. They were smaller than Julilly. They moved near her – their little bodies twitched like a wild bird she had caught once and held for a moment before it broke into flight.

Three men were ordered into a line behind the cart. They stood like broken trees, their hands dangling like willow branches in the wind. Julilly knew each one.

There was Ben, solid and strong and as black as midnight. He could chop a woodpile higher than his head when the others still had little mounds up to their knees.

There was kind, gentle Adam whose singing was low as the sightless hollow in a tree. And then there was Lester, the mulatto with speckly skin and angry eyes. Each one had a wife and one or two babies. They didn't move when the fat man with his puffed, oily fingers clamped a chain around their legs.

Julilly watched. The chain became a silver snake. It coiled over the ground, around the men, and up onto the back of their cart. It bit into a lock that held it fast.

Another strange white man led a work-horse in front of them. Julilly was afraid to look at him. She felt the tug and jerk of the wagon and the bounce of the man as he jumped onto the front seat.

'Gid-eee-up,' he cried, snapping the reins.

The snake-chain jingled in protest while the men, who were not used to it, tried to swing their bound legs in some sort of order. The fat man, with the toothpick still in his mouth, rode behind them on a smooth brown horse.

They moved down the dusty road, past the empty slave cabins and around by Master Hensen's house. It was empty. There were no curtains in the tall windows or chairs on the wide, shaded porch. Massa and Missy Hensen were gone.

Old John came through the wide front door, hobbled and bent. He shaded his eyes to watch the chain gang and the wagon load of children. When he saw Julilly, his back straightened. Pulling a large, white handkerchief from his pocket, he waved it up and down – up and down – until it became a tiny speck and disappeared.

Tears ran down Julilly's cheeks. She couldn't stop them, but she made no sound. The fat man didn't notice her.

1 What did the young girl have for breakfast?
2 What was Julilly's job on the plantation?
3 Make a list of the cruel acts that are committed in this extract.
4 Why do you think the slaves were being sold?
5 Suggest reasons why Mammy Sally wore a black head-bag on that particular day.
6 In what part of the United States do you think these events took place? Give reasons.
7 What would you say is the underlying tone or mood of this extract?
8 Imagine that you are Julilly. Describe what took place from your point of view, on that particular morning.
9 Write a short story describing the escape of the slaves during their wagon journey.

POETRY

► Beech tree

I planted in February
A bronze-leafed beech,
In the chill brown soil
I spread out its silken fibres.

Protected it from the goats
With wire netting
And fixed it firm against
The worrying wind.

Now it is safe, I said,
April must stir
My precious baby
To greenful loveliness.

It is August now, I have hoped
But I hope no more -
My beech tree will never hide sparrows
From hungry hawks.

Patrick Kavanagh

Questions

1 Why does Kavanagh refer to 'the chill brown soil'?
2 How did the poet protect his tree?
3 Explain clearly what the poet means in stanza three.
4 There is a mood of disappointment in stanza four. Why?
5 Pick out the images or phrases which you especially admire in this poem.
  Give your reasons.

PERSONAL AND FUNCTIONAL WRITING

1 You are a member of a fan club. Write an interesting **letter** to your
  favourite popstar/filmstar.

2 Write a **short story** ending with the words:
  'everybody is wise after the event'.

3 Write a **composition** on one of the following titles:
  (a) My life as a Pop star   (c)   An old house tells its story
  (b) The Third World war   (d)   Lost in a blizzard.

GRAMMAR

1 A reverse crossword puzzle
  Provide the clues for this puzzle by making definitions for the words.

Across
3
5
7
8
9
13
14
16
17

Down
1
2
3
4
6
10
11
12
14
15

Crossword grid:

1 O		2 S		3 A	R	4 C	H
5 F	I	6 L	L	E	D		A
	7 L	A	Y		8 E	B	B	S
		M			P		I
9 D	10 E	11 P	A	R	T	12 I	N	G
	V	B			T	
13 L	A	M	B	14 B	E	15 D
	D		16 E	N	A	M	E	L
17 V	E	R	Y		R		W

108

2 Correct one error in each of the following:
  (a) I didn't say nothing to vex him.
  (b) Either Mary or Peter are cheating.
  (c) They have did it a second time.

3 Write an interesting paragraph about any two of the following:
  cobbler, poacher, steeplejack, athlete, journalist, surgeon.

4 Replace each of the following by a single word:
  A person who hoards money
  A shop which sells ladies' fashions
  A bed on board a ship
  A person who stuffs birds and animals
  A person who goes abroad in search of work
  A fertile place in the desert

5 Write out the sentences in your copy and fill in the blank spaces with
  either *done* or *did*.
  He ____ most of his work in the office. He has not ____ his homework.
  When he ____ that he was punished. Who ____ that? They had not ____
  that for many years. Why have you ____ that? He ____ his best.

MEDIA STUDIES

1 Suggest a suitable caption for this photograph and say why you chose it.
2 What are your feelings when you look at this picture?
3 Imagine that you are an inhabitant of the town. Write a brief account of
  what is happening in the picture.

1 What is the most important feature of this advertisement in your opinion?
2 How are the caption and the photograph connected in this advertisement?
3 Write an appropriate speech bubble which you think conveys the girl's thoughts.
4 Glamorous young girls are regularly featured in advertisements. What are your views on this type of advertising?

UNIT 12

READING

➤ Prison escape

There were four screws in the yard, walking up and down with set, expressionless faces. And I knew there were two more watching from the high windows above my head. From there they could see into the street outside the exterior wall. God in heaven, surely they'd ring the alarm as soon as they saw that mechanical lift drive into the street. They couldn't be as stupid as all that.

The minutes went by. I found myself losing track of time. Fifteen minutes had already gone by – or was it only five? Again I could feel the sweat on the palms of my hands, and again I rubbed them dry. If I had to jump for a rope I didn't want any chance of slipping.

I looked at Cosgrave again. He was standing with his head cocked on one side listening to what Paddy had to say, and I saw him flick an eye towards me before he burst into a guffaw of laughter

and slapped Paddy on the back.

I didn't see him give the signal but suddenly there were raised voices at the other end of the yard, so perhaps the slap on Paddy's back had been the signal. I got to my feet and began to walk slowly forward as though hypnotised by that distant chalk mark. Slade pushed himself away from the wall and came forward, hobbling on his sticks.

The men all around me were looking towards the disturbance which had grown noisier. Some of the prisoners were running in that direction and the screws had begun to converge on the fight. I glanced to my right and saw Hudson, the senior screw, who had apparently sprung from nowhere, making his way across the yard. He wasn't running but walking at a smart pace, and he was on a collision course with me.

Something astonishing happened behind. There was a sharp crack, like a minor explosion and a billow of dense, white smoke erupted from the ground. I kept going but Hudson turned and stared. There were more explosions in the yard and the smoke grew thick and heavy. Somebody was being liberal with the smoke bombs that were being tossed over the wall.

Hudson was now behind me, and I heard his anguished bellow. 'Escape! Escape! Sound the alarm.'

Frantically he blew on his whistle but I kept going to where Slade was waiting. His face was set in lines of strain and as I approached he said urgently. 'Where the hell is that damned contraption?'

I looked up and saw it coming over through the wreaths of smoke, looming over the wall like the head and neck of a prehistoric monster with slimy weeds dripping from its jaws. As it dipped down I saw that the weeds were four knotted ropes dangling from the platform on which stood a man who was, so help me, talking into a telephone.

I bent down. 'Come on. Slade; up you go!'

He dropped his sticks as I heaved him up and he made a grab at one of the ropes as it came within reach. He was no lightweight and it was not easy for me to hold him up. He caught on to the rope and I was thankful when his weight eased from me.

The man on the platform was looking down at us and when he saw that Slade had a secure hold he spoke urgently into the telephone and the platform began to rise. The only trouble about that was it was leaving me behind. I made a frantic leap and grasped the last knot on the same rope that Slade was climbing.

He was going up fast but his legs were flailing about and he caught me under the jaw with the tip of his shoes. I felt dizzy and nearly let go but managed to tighten my grip at the last moment.

Then somebody grabbed my ankle and I looked down and saw it was Hudson, his face contorted with effort. The man had a grip like iron so I lifted my other leg and booted him in the face. I was learning from Slade already. He let go and tumbled to the ground which, by that time, seemed to be a long way down. I carried on up the rope, my shoulder muscles cracking, until I could grasp the edge of the platform.

Slade was sprawled on the steel floor, gasping with the effort he had made, and the man with the telephone bent down. 'Stay there,' he said. 'You'll be all right.' He spoke into the mouthpiece again.

I looked down and saw the barbed wire apparently moving away underneath as the great articulated arm swept me over the wall. Then it began to drop and the man bent down again, directing his words at both of us. 'Do exactly as I do,' he said calmly.

We were swept dizzily over the street and then stopped dead. A small open delivery truck came from nowhere and pulled up beneath the platform. The man swung over the railings of the platform and dropped lightly into the back of the truck and I thankfully let go of the rope and followed him. Slade came after and fell on top of me and I cursed him, but then he was thrown off me by a sudden surge of acceleration as the little truck took off and went round the first corner with a squeal of tyres.

Desmond Bagley *The Freedom Trap*

uestions

1   What physical evidence is there of the narrator's tension as the escape time approached?
2   What was the probable purpose of the fight in the prison yard?
3   What was the most difficult part of the escape attempt for the two prisoners?
4   Why was the open delivery truck a vital element in the escape attempt?
5   What evidence is there to suggest that the plan was very well organised?
6   'God in heaven, surely they'd ring the alarm'.
    What does this sentence suggest about the narrator's state of mind at that moment?
7   Why do you think the faces of the four 'screws' were 'set' and 'expressionless'?
8   'Like the head and neck of a prehistoric monster...'
    Do you think this is an apt description? Explain why.
9   Write an imaginary conversation between the two escaping prisoners as they sat in the back of the delivery truck during their dash for freedom.

1   Suggest a suitable title for this picture and say why you chose it.
2   How would you describe the expression on the woman's face?
3   Describe how this picture makes you feel.
4   For what purposes could this picture be used? Give reasons.

We can also secure your peace of mind.

Since 1975, Pandoro has been operating on the Irish Sea, steadfastly acquiring a reputation for professionalism and reliability.

And since 1975, Pandoro has steadily been gaining the confidence of freight managers and truck drivers - thanks to its superior range and level of services. You see, with Pandoro, you can opt for door-to-door, quay-to-quay, accompanied or unaccompanied freight services on all routes. And because ours is exclusively a freight service, drivers are not expected to get in line with holidaymakers, meaning less delays and less re-scheduling headaches in high season. In short, with Pandoro, you're secure in the knowledge that the freight experts are behind you.

Pandoro

Make it your link to the European business world.
Pandoro Ltd., Tolka Quay, Dublin 1. Tel: (01) 8745001. Fax: 8366323.
Pandoro Ltd., Dock Street, Fleetwood, Lancashire. FY7 6HR. Tel/Fax: (0253) 777111.

1 Do you think this is a good advertisement? Explain why.
2 Where would you expect to find this type of advertisement?
3 Comment on the effectiveness of the caption at the top of the advertisement.
4 The artist focuses your attention on the chain. Why do you think she does this?

- Select any **short story** which you have studied which deals with animals or nature.
- Write a brief account of the happenings and explain clearly why this particular story appeals to you.

PERSONAL AND FUNCTIONAL WRITING

1 You are looking for a job. Read the following advertisements, choose one, and write a **letter** of application for the position.

GARDENER/CARETAKER

required for country house South Leinster.
Own self contained flat.
Must be capable driver. Other daily staff kept. Refs. essential.
Please reply with CV and copy refs. to:
Box 8500 X.

BUILDERS LABOURER/ HANDYMAN REQUIRED

By Contractor in the Midland area
Apply, giving details of last working experience to
Box No. 9999 G

Part-Time Work in your own area

Sell SkinPerfect Cosmetics

from our fantastic new catalogue
Cosmetics Skin and Body Care, Children's Products plus Royal Jelly Range and High Fashion Costume Jewellery and Special Christmas Range
If interested you can earn high commission plus free products and prizes
For full details please reply to Box No. 7900 X

---

2 Write a **report**, suitable for a school magazine, in which you describe a football or basketball final won by your college.

3 Write a **composition** on one of the following titles:
(a) A bank robbery
(b) An exciting event in history
(c) Important inventions
(d) Visiting the dentist

GRAMMAR

1 Punctuate the following passage:
whats the matter with you today asked the foreman my back is hurting me replied john i think i should go home and have a rest if you go home you can stay there two other men are looking for your job i think ill try to keep going so said john exercise might be good for my back

2 Form abstract nouns from the following list of verbs:

| agree | refuse | direct | compose | defend |
| suspect | persist | notify | inflame | oppose |

3 Correct one error in each of the following:
(a) They all came accept your sister.
(b) Monkies are very amusing animals.
(c) Give me them books.

4 Write out in your copy the following list of words with the correct words in the spaces:

you break	you broke	you have broken
you awake	_____	_____
you choose	_____	_____
you begin	_____	_____
you fly	_____	_____
you go	_____	_____
you shake	_____	_____
you swim	_____	_____
you draw	_____	_____

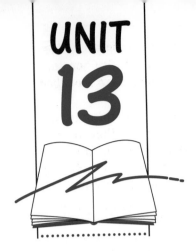

UNIT 13

READING

► Bob-a-job

'Cooler today,' said David, appearing in the front garden. 'Coming over to Warren Hill?'

Kim paused, half in, half out of the gate, went back and leaned against the wall. 'Do you mind if we don't, today? I thought I'd go odd-jobbing. I could do with a bit of extra pocket money.'

David considered this for a moment, and said: 'Not a bad idea. I could use some extra holiday money, come to that. Hang on a tick and I'll come with you.' He vanished indoors. Kim waited, pleased but surprised. The Holder children were very rarely short of cash. Still – knocking on strangers' doors was always *much* better when there were two of you. Particularly when you were trying to part them from their money.

'This,' said David, 'is my anti-mugger jacket. Secret inside pocket. By the time they find it you'll have had time to walk to the police station and back.'

'And you'll be lying in a pool of blood... d'you really think we're going to get enough to make us worth mugging?'

'No harm in hoping. I'll store the takings in the pocket and we'll split it when we've finished. O.K.?'

'O.K.. Hey' – as David turned purposefully to the right, into Broadmeadow Lane – 'where are you going? What's the matter with *this* road?'

'Everybody who ever goes scrounging knows that *the* place to go is Addison Avenue. We'll make twice as much there in half the time. Raffle ticket sellers – Oxfam – carol singers – penny for the guy – they throng there in their thousands.'

'Join the happy throng. I hope they've got some money left, that's all.'

'The great thing about Addison Avenue is that they've *always* got money left. Kim – by the way – I'm so sorry about your mother's job.'

'How the hell do you know about that?' Kim said grumpily.

'My mother saw your mother last night in the off-licence. She told her. She

118
▼

said you were celebrating it.' Mrs Holder had been no more fooled by Mrs Tate's gaiety than had Kim; she told David, who entirely agreed with her, that Mrs Tate was a *superb* lady. And very courageous. 'You do seem to have bad luck, Kim.'

'We do not!' Kim swung round in amazement; what a peculiar thing to say. And then she remembered what David thought about her father; he saw that she remembered, and neither of them said any more about it.

They began at the beginning, with the first house. Nobody was in. 'That's the catch,' David said. 'They all spend the summer on the Riviera.'

'Let's come back at Christmas and sing carols.'

'People only pay carol singers to make them go away. Why wait till Christmas? It would work just as well now. Better.' They marched up the next path singing *O Come All Ye Faithful*. The door was opened by a tall, severe-looking man of about seventy.

'What's this?' David explained. 'Bob a job! Ha.' He looked at Kim. 'You don't look much like a Boy Scout.'

'I'm a civilian,' said Kim.

'Air Force,' said the man, with pride. 'Battle of Britain. Those were the days. What this country needs is another war!' David looked disgusted; Kim began to hum *God Rest Ye Merry, Gentlemen*, softly.

'Lawn needs mowing,' said the man. 'At the back. That the sort of thing you had in mind? Good. Lawnmower in the shed. Mind my wife.'

'When the Russians nuke us,' Kim said, 'he'll die laughing.' They found his wife dozing in a garden chair, plum in the middle of the lawn, which did need mowing, badly. The wife opened her eyes, and looked alarmed. David explained again.

'But the mower's broken!' she said. 'It's been broken for weeks. I'd suggest that you borrowed next door's, but they've gone to the Riviera. I know what you could do, though. There's a flower-bed beyond the rockery that needs weeding. I keep meaning to do it, but my back's not what it was.'

It was not a large bed, and there were two of them; it was soon done.

'I never handle money,' said the wife. 'You'll have to see my husband about that.'

'Weeding, eh?' he said, when they presented themselves once more at the front door. 'Step inside a moment, young man. Can't talk finances with a woman. Hopeless. They haven't a clue.' David nodded solemnly and said 'Quite right.' Kim remained, fuming, on the doorstep. The man looked David up and down, asked if he played cricket, was told yes, and gave him a pound.

'The old rat,' said Kim.

'Nobody's told him you've been liberated.' David, clearly, found it very funny. Kim glared at him.

'How much did he give us anyway? Ten pence? Twenty? Does he actually know about decimal currency?'

'Two quid. Can't complain about that.'

Questions

1 How do you know that David's family is better off than Kim's?
2 Kim's mother said that they were 'celebrating it'. What was 'it' and do you think they really celebrated?
3 How do you know that Kim's father is no longer at home?
4 Explain why Kim was angry.
5 What evidence is there in the extract to suggest that the residents of Addison Avenue are wealthy?
6 Can you find any evidence in the extract which suggests that David was a generous boy?
7 Why do you think David was disgusted by the man's comments?
8 People in this extract show that they have different attitudes to women. Explain this statement by referring to two of the characters in the story.
9 Have you ever done odd jobs for other people in order to earn pocket money? Write a short account of an unusual or amusing incident which happened to you while you were doing so.

1   Suggest a suitable title for this photograph and give reasons for your
    choice.
2   Imagine that you are watching the launching of this shuttle. Write a brief
    but vivid description of the occasion.
3   Orbiting satellites have a variety of uses. List some of them.
4. Many people are totally opposed to the spending of billions of pounds each
    year on space exploration. What are your views?

AT LAST - SOMETHING KIDS LOVE THAT'S GOOD FOR THEM.

The new Reach Wonder Grip toothbrush is a hit with kids - and their parents too. Reach Wonder Grip's unique handle makes it easy for kids to hold, and its state-of-the-art rubber thumb guide ensures proper brushing. Clinical tests prove that Reach Wonder Grip cleans better, even those hard to reach back teeth - the most serious test of all.

And since kids enjoy brushing with Reach Wonder Grip more than other toothbrushes, you can see why Reach Wonder Grip is quite seriously, a better way for kids to brush. From Johnson & Johnson.

REACH WONDER GRIP™

Johnson & Johnson

1   Advertisements always have a target audience in mind. At whom is this advertisement aimed and why?
2   What features of this advertisement are calculated to capture the readers attention?
3   Why do you think a cartoon design is used rather than a normal photograph?
4   Suggest how this advertisement might be improved.

➤ **Song of the Battery Hen**

We can't grumble about accommodation:
we have a new concrete floor that's
always dry, four walls that are
painted white, and a sheet-iron roof
the rain drums on. A fan blows warm air
beneath our feet to disperse the smell
of chicken-shit and, on dull days,
fluorescent lighting sees us.

You can tell me: if you come by
the North door, I am in the twelfth pen
on the left-hand side of the third row
from the floor; and in that pen
I am usually the middle one of three.
But, even without directions, you'd
discover me. I have had same orange-
red comb, yellow beak and auburn
feathers, but as the door opens and you
hear above the electric fan a kind of
one-word wail, I am the one
who sounds loudest in my head.

Listen. Outside this house there's an
orchard with small moss-green apple
trees; beyond that, two fields of
cabbages; then, on the far side of
the road, a broiler house. Listen:
one cockerel crows out of there, as
tall and proud as the first hour of sun.
Sometimes I stop calling with the others
to listen, and wonder if he hears me.
The next time you come here, look for me.
Notice the way I sound inside my head.
God made us all quite differently,
and blessed us with this expensive home

Edwin Brock

uestions

1. Does the hen like the accommodation provided? Give reasons for your answer.
2. What do you think is the worst feature of the hen's existence?
3. From the evidence of the poem, what is the poet's attitude to battery egg production?
4. How would you describe the tone of the poem? Why?
5. In this poem, Edwin Brock imagines what it is really like to be a captive animal. Write a short extract in which another animal describes what it is like to be held in captivity.

PERSONAL AND FUNCTIONAL WRITING

1. You won a trip to the Olympic Games and were present when an Irish athlete won a gold medal. Write a **letter** to your parents describing the occasion. Include the following details:
   huge crowds; great atmosphere; flags waving; deafening noise; moment of victory; medal presentation; National Anthem; proud to be Irish.

2. You have witnessed the theft of an old lady's handbag by two youngsters as she walked along the street. The police have asked you for details. Write a **report** of the incident. Include as much detail as possible.

3. Write a **composition** on one of the following titles:
   (a) Hobbies
   (b) A plane crash
   (c) Walking to school on a frosty morning
   (d) A visit to a foreign country

GRAMMAR

1. Write a short sentence describing clearly what each of the following does:

a blacksmith	a cobbler	a greengrocer	an architect
an angler	a newsagent	a mechanic	an author
a surgeon	a chemist	a detective	a carpenter

2. Correct one error in each of the following:
   (a) The conductor asked for my fair.
   (b) Your not supposed to do that.

3. Punctuate the following passage:
   have you ever read huckleberry finn by the american author mark twain asked the teacher i dont think so replied michael here it is then said the teacher you'll enjoy it

4. Make the following words plural:

monkey	tooth	negro	thief	cigarette	school
edge	victory	deer	fly	country	mousetrap
copy	man	calf	wife	armchair	poet
match	trousers	tomato	friend	eye	inch

READING

➤ A hunting accident

The fox was running easily. He came up the hill through the short wet grass, dropped into a ditch and ran up through the flowing water. The ditch was deep, overgrown with hawthorn and overhung with enormous elms whose last yellow leaves were gleaming against the sky; a wet, November sky, heavy over the hill and over the brimming, water-streaked valley below.

A man hedging saw the fox break cover a hundred yards along and streak away over the adjoining pasture. For a moment it was silhouetted on the crest of the hill, a big dog-fox that had played the game before. The man hedging sniffed, and rested his billhook. In his leather jacket and muddy breeches he was invisible in the shadow of the hedge. He would watch and say nothing. 'They'll get no help from me,' he was thinking. 'Or as much as I get from them, which is the same thing. See all, say nowt.' The thought gave him a nice satisfaction, to break the monotony of hedging from dawn till dark.

Hounds were not long appearing. They poured through the hedge in the lower pasture and came up the hill all in a bunch, making a noise which stirred the stomach of the hedging man, for all his sour thoughts. Even the huntsman was not up with them, and the field was strung out across half a mile of grazing below. The pack of hounds tumbled and scrambled into the hawthorn and broke up momentarily, some bursting out into the far field, some casting along the hawthorn roots. Swirling, yelping, the smooth wave checked, like water dividing among rocks; then an excited tongue from down the ditch drew it together again. The lost, bounding novices wheeled to follow, launching themselves frantically back into the muddy ditch; a splashing, a cracking of branches, a shower of dying leaves like gold pennies and hounds were away, tumbling out into the open with the scent high in their nostrils.

As the clamour died away, the hedging man was conscious of the respite, hearing them go, waiting for what he knew was coming. He shrank back, brown against the brown elm trunks. The air stank of rotting leaves, the musk

125
▼

of the fox. He had seen it all before, the hedger, and knew how his own common sense became over-ruled. Already the thud of hoofs was in his bootsoles. He braced himself, his knuckles tight on the billhook, and watched the spots of red burst out of the trees below. Check, wheel: he could see the score marks of iron-shod hoofs in the wet grass, then the pounding in the hillside like its own heart beating and the first breast of a big bay horse in his vision, its breath roaring, the huntsman shouting his encouragement as he viewed hounds on the far slope. The man was glancing round for a way through. There was a gate at the far end, but a wasting of precious ground to go through it; the hedger knew the man would jump, and there was only one possibility: a slight gap in the hawthorn and the ditch deep and ugly below, the approach uphill.

The huntsman went through, holding his arm up as the bare twigs thrust at him. The phalanx of riders behind, pounding up the hill, snarled up, separating, some making for the gate, some for the gap, and cursing anyone in their way. The ground shook to the uphill gallop of lathered, shining horses, foam on their bits, eyes frenzied with excitement. Only the thrusters made for the gap: there was a shouting of advice, some doubt, and a horse pulled up in a great flurry of mud for a sudden failing of courage on the part of his rider. The horse behind was crossed and its rider swore. He was just a boy, but his swearing, and the fury in his eyes, were those of a man. He gave his baulked horse a crack with his whip and went for the gap at an angle, when any sane man would have gone back for a fresh approach. The horse made a desperate leap and in mid-air its rider was twisting round, shouting behind him: 'Come on, Will! It's all right! There were only three horses to follow, most of the field having opted for the gate, and of these the leader was a grey, whose rider was also a boy, even younger than the one in front. The grey, its nostrils red with blood, its eyes wild with excitement, pounded towards the gap on the tail of its stable-mate, and the boy on top hadn't the strength to change its course. That he wanted to was evident. Unlike the boy in front, his face was closed with fear. Sweat and mud streaked a greenish pallor. His dark eyes, seeing the hedge loom, flared with terror. He flung himself forward, his fingers twisting in the horse's mane, reins flying, but the horse jumped even bigger than the boy was expecting. His seat, the grip of his thin legs, were not enough to hold the boldness of the big, peppered grey gelding; the twigs whipped the boy's face and he fell backwards and sideways through the cracking branches and heavily into the bottom of the ditch. The grey scarcely felt its loss, landed in a smother of flying mud and galloped on.

K. M. Peyton *Flambards*

1 Why was the ditch useful to the fox?
2 How could the hedger tell that the riders were approaching?
3 What happened to anger one of the boy riders when he reached the hedge?
4 For what reason did the boy called Will fail in the jump?
5 Why do you think the hedger decided not to tell the hunters where the fox was?
6 What evidence is there to suggest that, at the moment when the hedger saw the hounds, some of them had lost the fox's scent?
7 What impressions are conveyed to you by the description of the valley as 'brimming' and 'water-streaked'?
8 List five words or phrases which describe the actions of the hounds as they searched for the fox.
9 Read this extract again and compare it with John Masefield's poem 'Reynard the Fox' in Unit 15.
   Which description of the hunt do you prefer? Give your reasons.

WHAT I HAVE READ

- Choose one **short story** which deals with some aspect of life in a rural area, and one **short story** which deals with life in a city or town.
- Give the titles of the stories and name the authors.
- Write a brief account of one of the stories.
- Which of these stories do you prefer? Give reasons for your answer.

PERSONAL AND FUNCTIONAL WRITING

1 Write a **letter** of application in reply to one of the following newspaper advertisements. Give details of your age, education and other relevant information.
   (a) Required, respectable young person to train as shop assistant. Excellent prospects for suitable candidate. Box 412 *The Irish Press*.
   (b) Applications are invited for the position of Sales Representative with expanding computer organisation. Apply in writing Box 724 *The Irish Times*.

2   Write a **short story** beginning with the words: 'Despite the bad weather forecast, we set out to climb the mountain'.

3   Write a **composition** on one of the following titles:
   (a) Life in a large city
   (b) Pollution and its consequences
   (c) A plane crash
   (d) Little brothers (sisters) are a nuisance

☐ GRAMMAR

1   Write down the opposite of the following words by adding a prefix:
   behave   legible   connect   correct   regular
   trust   wise   fire   modest   audible

2   All the following words have more than one meaning. Find as many meanings as you can for each of them, and then write sentences to show you know each meaning.
   scale   punch   note   miss   stand
   lock   form   element   down   train

3   Write out the sentences in your copy and fill in the spaces with either *its* or *it's*.
   ____ a long way to Tipperary. Gold never loses ____ value. ____ the first house on the right. ____ no use saying you're sorry. When I looked at the monkey ____ teeth were clenched and ____ eyes were shining. This year ____ hardly ever stopped raining.

4   Punctuate the following passage:
   i wouldnt mind going to see superman said donal but i havent the money il pay for you this time said peter thats no good replied donal id have to pay for you the next time.

1   Where do you think this photograph was taken? Why?
2   Suggest a suitable caption for the picture and give reasons for your choice.
3   'This picture is one of contrasts'. In what ways is this statement true?
4   What are your views on the work done by Irish people on the missions?

YOU CAN'T TAKE THEM BACK IF THEY START TO HURT.

A child's foot is a precious object.

Its twenty-six bones are soft, delicate and easily damaged. Not just in those first
unsteady steps, but in every stride and stomp of childhood. In fact,
the bones won't harden fully until around the age of eighteen. Sad to report, 70% of
all children have damaged feet by the age of thirteen.

We, at Clarks, know many of these problems are avoidable, simply by ensuring your
child's shoes fit properly. So we insist our shoes are fitted by a
trained assistant. The shoes come in half sizes and up to four width fittings, not just
for little ones but for older children too. For healthy growth, we always
allow up to three months' growing room. Our leather uppers allow the feet to breathe.

Of course, you can always find a cheaper pair of shoes.

But you'll never find another pair of feet.

Clarks

For more information on caring for children's feet call Freephone 0800 616427.   Growing feet in safe hands.

---

1   How does this advertisement try to convince the reader?
2   The advertisement does not include a photograph or props. Does this make
    it less effective? What is your opinion?
3   What do you think is the key phrase or sentence in the advertisement?
4   Would this advertisement persuade you to purchase the product? Explain
    your answer.

DRAMA

THE MERCHANT OF VENICE

This extract is taken from Act Four of The Merchant of Venice
by William Shakespeare.

Antonio has failed to repay his debt to Shylock, the Jewish moneylender.
Portia, dressed as a lawyer, tries in vain to persuade Shylock not to demand
his pound of flesh.

[EXTRACT]

Antonio:	Most heartily I do beseech the court To give the judgement.
Portia:	Why then, thus it is: You must prepare your bosom for his knife. Therefore lay bare your bosom.
Shylock:	Ay, his breast: 'Nearest his heart": those are the very words.
Portio:	It is so. Are there balance here to weigh the flesh?
Shylock:	I have them ready.
Portia:	Have by some surgeon, Shylock, on your charge To stop his wounds, lest he do bleed to death.
Shylock:	Is it so nominated in the bond?
Portia:	It is not so expressed: but what of that? 'Twere good you do so much for charity.
Shylock:	I cannot find it; 'tis not in the bond.
Portia:	You, merchant, have you anything to say?
Antonio:	But little: I am armed and well prepared. Give me your hand, Bassanio: fare you well! Grieve not that I am fallen to this for you; Commend me to your honourable wife: Tell her the process of Antonio's end;

Say how I love you, speak me fair in death;
And, when the tale is told, bid her be judge
Whether Bassanio had not once a love.

Bassanio: Antonio, I am married to a wife
Which is as dear to me as life itself;
But life itself, my wife, and all the world,
Are not with me esteemed above thy life:
I would lose all, ay, sacrifice them all
Here to this devil, to deliver you.

Portia: Your wife would give you little thanks for that,
If she were by, to hear you make the offer.

Shylock: We trifle time: I pray thee, pursue sentence.

Portia: A pound of that same merchant's flesh is thine?
The court awards it, and the law doth give it.

Shylock: Most rightful judge!

Portia: And you must cut this flesh from off his breast:
The law allows it and the court awards it.

Shylock: Most learned judge! A sentence!
(*to Antonio*) Come, prepare!

Portia: Tarry a little, there is something else, –
This bond doth give thee here no jot of blood,
The words expressly are 'a pound of flesh':
Take then thy bond, take thou thy pound of flesh,
But in the cutting it, if thou dost shed
One drop of Christian blood, thy lands and goods
Are, by the laws of Venice, confiscate
Unto the state of Venice.

Questions

1 Portia shows herself to be a person of considerable ability and intelligence. Explain by reference to the extract how this statement is true.

2 From the evidence of this extract what type of person do you imagine Shylock to be?

3 How would you describe Antonio's character as it is revealed in the extract?

4 Bassanio says that he would sacrifice everything to save Antonio. Why do you think he is willing to do this?

5 Explain what type of stage setting would best suit this extract. Refer to such items as props, costumes, lighting, position of actors, etc.

JUNO AND THE PAYCOCK

This extract is taken from the opening scene of Juno and the Paycock
by Sean O'Casey.
It is set in the slums of Dublin during the Irish Civil War.
We are introduced to Mrs. Boyle (Juno), her daughter Mary and son Johnny.
It is the early forenoon and Mary is reading a newspaper.

[EXTRACT]

MRS. BOYLE. Isn't he come in yet?

MARY. No, Mother.

MRS. BOYLE. Oh, he'll come in when he likes; struttin' about the town like a paycock with Joxer, I suppose. I hear all about Mrs. Tancred's son is in this mornin's paper.

MARY. The full details are in it this mornin'; seven wounds he had – one entherin' the neck, with an exit wound beneath the left shoulder-blade; another in the left breast penethratin' the heart, an'...

JOHNNY. (*springing up from the fire*). Oh, quit that readin', for God's sake! Are yous losin' all your feelin's? It'll soon be that none of yous'll read anythin' that's not about butcherin'!

He goes quickly into the room on left

MARY. He's gettin' very sensitive, all of a sudden!

MRS. BOYLE. I'll read it myself, Mary, by an' by, when I come home. Everybody's sayin' that he was a Die-hard – thanks be to God that Johnny had nothin' to do with him this long time...(*Opening the parcel and taking out some sausages, which she places on a plate*) Ah, then, if that father o' yours doesn't come in soon for his breakfast, he may go without any; I'll not wait much longer for him.

MARY. Can't you let him get it himself when he comes in?

MRS. BOYLE. Yes, an' let him bring in Joxer Daly along with him? Ay, that's what he'd like, an' that's what he's waitin' for – till he thinks I'm gone to work, an' then sail in with the boul' Joxer, to burn all the coal an' dhrink all the tea in the place, to show them what a good Samaritan he is! But I'll stop here till he comes in, if I have to wait till to-morrow mornin'.

VOICE OF JOHNNY INSIDE. Mother!

MRS. BOYLE. Yis?

VOICE OF JOHNNY. Bring us in a dhrink o' wather.

MRS. BOYLE. Bring in that fella a dhrink o' wather, for God's sake, Mary.

MARY. Isn't he big an' able enough to come out an' get it himself?

MRS. BOYLE. If you weren't well yourself you'd like somebody to bring you in a dhrink o' wather. [*She brings in drink and returns.*]

MRS. BOYLE.	Isn't it terrible to have to be waitin' this way! You'd think he was bringin' twenty poun's a week into the house the way he's going on. He wore out the Health Insurance long ago, he's afther wearin' out the unemployment dole, an' now he's thryin' to wear out me! An' constantly singin', no less, when he ought always to be on his knees offerin' up a Novena for a job!
MARY.	*(tying a ribbon fillet-wise around her head).* I don't like this ribbon, ma; I think I'll wear the green – it looks betther than the blue.
MRS. BOYLE.	Ah. wear whatever ribbon you like, girl, only don't be botherin' me. I don't know what a girl on strike wants to be wearin' a ribbon round her head for or silk stockin's on her legs either; it's wearin' them things that make the employers think they're givin' yous too much money.
MARY.	The hour is past now when we'll ask the employers' permission to wear what we like.
MRS. BOYLE.	I don't know why you wanted to walk out for Jennie Claffey; up to this you never had a good word for her.
MARY.	What's the use of belongin' to a Trades Union if you won't stand up for your principles? Why did they sack her? It was a clear case of victimisation. We couldn't let her walk the streets, could we?
MRS. BOYLE.	No, of course yous couldn't – yous wanted to keep her company. Wan victim wasn't enough. When the employers sacrifice wan victim, the Trades Unions go wan betther be sacrifin' a hundred.
MARY.	It doesn't matther what you say, ma – a principle's a principle.
MRS. BOYLE.	Yis; an' when I go into oul' Murphy's to-morrow, an' he gets to know that, instead o' paying' all, I'm goin' to borry more, what'll he say when I tell him a principle's a principle? What'll we do if he refuses to give us any more on tick?

Questions

1 What do you think Mrs. Boyle means when she describes her husband as: 'Struttin' about the town like a paycock"?
2 How would you describe the language used in this extract? Support the points you make by suitable reference.
3 Life was very difficult for families living in the tenements of Dublin at this time. Where is there evidence of this in the extract?
4 How would you describe Johnny's reaction to the newspaper report of the killing of Mrs. Tancred's son? Suggest reasons why he may have reacted in this way.
5 Write a character sketch of Mrs. Boyle as she appears in this extract.

ROMEO AND JULIET

The play Romeo and Juliet *by William Shakespeare tells the tragic tale of the love affair between Romeo, a Montague, and Juliet, a Capulet.*

The two families have been deadly enemies for many years. In this extract, taken from Act I of the play, Romeo sees Juliet for the first time. Tybalt is a nephew of Capulet's wife.

[EXTRACT]

ROMEO	What lady is that which doth enrich the hand Of yonder knight?
SERVINGMAN	I know not, sir.
ROMEO	O! she doth teach the torches to burn bright. It seems she hangs upon the cheek of night Like a rich jewel in an Ethiop's ear; Beauty too rich for use, for earth too dear! So shows a snowy dove trooping with crows, As yonder lady o'er her fellows shows. The measure done, I'll watch her place of stand, And, touching hers, make blessed my rude hand Did my heart love till now? Forswear it, sight! For I ne'er saw true beauty till this night.
TYBALT	This, by his voice, should be a Montague. Fetch me my rapier, boy. What! dares the slave Come hither, cover'd with an antick face, To fleer and scorn at our solemnity? Now, by the stock and honour of my kin, To strike him dead I hold it not a sin.
CAPULET	Why, how now, kinsman! Wherefore storm you so?
TYBALT	Uncle, this is a Montague, our foe; A villain that is hither come in spite, To scorn at our solemnity this night.
CAPULET	Young Romeo, is it?
TYBALT	'Tis he, that villain Romeo.
CAPULET	Content thee, gentle coz, let him alone; He bears him like a portly gentleman; And, to say truth, Verona brags of him To be a virtuous and well-govern'd youth. I would not for the wealth of all this town Here in my house do him disparagement; Therefore be patient, take no note of him. It is my will, the which if thou respect, Show a fair presence and put off these frowns, An ill-beseeming semblance for a feast
TYBALT	It fits, when such a villain is a guest; I'll not endure him.

CAPULET	He shall be endur'd
	What! goodman boy, I say, he shall, go to,
	Am I the master here, or you? go to,
	You'll not endure him! God shall mend my soul!
	You'll make a mutiny among my guests!
	You will sit cock-a-hoop! You'll be the man!
TYBALT	Why, uncle, 'tis a shame
CAPULET	Go to, go to,
	You are a saucy boy – is't so indeed? –
	This trick may chance to scathe you. – I know what.
	You must contrary me! marry, 'tis time.
	Well said, my hearts! You are a princox, go:
	Be quiet, or – More light, more light! – For shame!
	I'll make you quiet. What! Cheerly, my hearts!
TYBALT	Patience perforce with wilful choler meeting
	Makes my flesh tremble in their different greeting.
	I will withdraw, but this intrusion shall
	Now seeming sweet convert to bitter gall.
	Exit.

Questions

1 Comment on the language used by Romeo in this extract. What does it tell us about his character?

2 From the evidence of this extract what type of person do you imagine Tybalt to be? Explain your answer.

3 Capulet shows considerable strength of character in this scene. Support this statement with evidence from the extract.

4 Capulet and Tybalt give us two totally contrasting pictures of Romeo. Give some examples which illustrate this point.

5 Describe the scenery or setting which in your opinion, would best suit this extract, position of the actors on stage, lighting, costumes, etc.

ABRAHAM LINCOLN

In this extract taken from the play Abraham Lincoln *by John Drinkwater, we
see the President in conversation with two ladies, Mrs Blow and Mrs Otherly,
whose attitudes to the American Civil War differ greatly.*

[EXTRACT]

LINCOLN:	Oh! good afternoon, ladies.
MRS OTHERLY:	Good afternoon, Mr President.
LINCOLN:	Good afternoon, good afternoon.
MRS BLOW:	And is there any startling news, Mr President?
LINCOLN:	Madam, every morning when I wake up, and say to myself, a hundred, or two hundred, or a thousand of my countrymen will be killed today, I find it startling.
MRS BLOW:	Oh yes, to be sure. But I mean, is there any good news?
LINCOLN:	Yes. There is news of victory. They lost twenty-seven hundred men – we lost eight hundred.
MRS BLOW:	How splendid.
LINCOLN:	Thirty-five hundred.
MRS BLOW:	Oh, but you mustn't talk like that. Mr President. There were only eight hundred that mattered.
LINCOLN:	The world is larger than your heart, Madam.
MRS BLOW:	Now the dear President is becoming whimsical, Mrs Lincoln.
MRS OTHERLY:	Mr President.
LINCOLN:	Yes, ma'am.
MRS OTHERLY:	I don't like to impose upon your hospitality. I know how difficult everything is for you. But one has to take one's opportunities. May I ask you a question?
LINCOLN:	Certainly, ma'am.
MRS OTHERLY:	Isn't is possible for you to stop this war? In the name of a suffering country, I ask you that.
MRS BLOW:	I'm sure such a question would never have entered my head.
LINCOLN:	It is a perfectly right question. Ma'am, I have but one thought always – how can this thing be stopped? But we must ensure the integrity of the Union. In two years, war has become an hourly bitterness to me. I believe I suffer no less than any man. But it must be endured. The cause was a right one two years ago. It is unchanged.
MRS OTHERLY:	I know you are noble and generous. But I believe that war must be wrong under any circumstances, for any cause.

MRS BLOW: I'm afraid the President would have but little encouragement if he listened often to this kind of talk.

LINCOLN: I beg you not to harass yourself, madam. Ma'am, I too believe war to be wrong. It is the weakness and the jealousy and the folly of men that make a thing so wrong possible. But we are all weak, and jealous, and foolish. That's how the world is, ma'am, and we cannot outstrip the world. Some of the worst of us are sullen, aggressive still – just clumsy, greedy pirates. Some of us have grown out of that. But the best of us have an instinct to resist aggression if it won't listen to persuasion. You may say it's a wrong instinct. I don't know. But it's there, and it's there in millions of good men. I don't believe it's a wrong instinct. I believe that the world must come to wisdom slowly. It is for us who hate aggression to persuade men always and earnestly against it, and hope that, little by little, they will hear us. But in the meantime there will come moments when the aggressors will force the instinct to resistance to act. Then we must act earnestly, praying always in our courage that never again will this thing happen. And then we must turn again, and again, and again to persuasion. This appeal to force is the misdeed of an imperfect world. But we are imperfect. We must strive to purify the world, but we must not think ourselves pure above the world. When I had this thing to decide, it would have been easy to say, 'No, I will have none of it; it is evil, and I will not touch it.' But that would have decided nothing, and I saw what I believed to be the truth as I now put it to you, ma'am. It's a forlorn thing for any man to have this responsibility in his heart. I may see wrongly, but that's how I see it.

MRS OTHERLY: Thank you, Mr President, for what you've said. I must try to think about it. But I always believed war to be wrong. I didn't want my boy to go because I believed war to be wrong. But he would. This paper came to me last week. From his Colonel. You may read it, Mr Lincoln.

LINCOLN: 'Dear Madam, I regret to inform you that...' Ma'am, there are times when no man may speak. I grieve for you, I grieve for you.

MRS OTHERLY: I think I will go. You don't mind my saying what I did?

LINCOLN: We are all poor creatures, ma'am. Think kindly of me. Mary, will you...?

MRS LINCOLN: Of course, Abraham. Mrs Otherly...

MRS BLOW: Of course it's very sad for her, poor woman. But she makes her trouble worse by these perverted views, doesn't she? And, I hope you will show no signs of weakening, Mr President, till it has been made impossible for those shameful rebels to hold up their heads again. Goliath says you ought to make a proclamation that no mercy will be shown to them afterwards. I'm sure I shall never speak to one of them again. Well I must be going. I'll see Mrs Lincoln as I go out. Good afternoon, Mr President.

LINCOLN: Good afternoon, madam. And I'd like to offer ye a word of advice. That poor mother told me what she thought. I don't agree with her, but I honour her. She's wrong, but she is noble. You've told me what you think. I don't agree with you, and I'm ashamed of you and your like. You, who have sacrificed nothing, babble about destroying the South while other people conquer it. I accepted this war with a sick heart, and I've a heart that's near to breaking every day. I accepted it in the name of humanity, and just and merciful dealing, and the hope of love and charity on earth. And you come to me, talking of revenge and destruction, and malice, and enduring hate. These gentle people are mistaken, but they are mistaken cleanly, and in a great name. It is you that dishonour the cause for which we stand – it is you who would make it a mean and little thing. Good afternoon.

from *Abraham Lincoln* by John Drinkwater.

uestions

1 What is the real meaning of Lincoln's comments when he says: 'Thirty-five hundred"?
2 Explain the sentence 'The world is larger than your heart, Madam'.
3 What does President Lincoln mean when he says 'Ma'am, there are times when no man may speak"?
4 Describe in your own words the attitude of Mrs Blow towards the Southern rebels.
5 What is Lincoln's attitude to Mrs Blow?
6 Write a character sketch of Mrs Otherly.
7 Give, in your own words, the attitude of President Lincoln towards war.
8 In what circumstances, if any, do you feel that war is justifiable? Explain your reasons.

UNIT 15

READING

➤ The future

According to the travel industry's experts we will all be taking three or four holidays a year. 'Theme' holidays, like the ones offered by Walt Disney World Florida, will be popular.

There was a feature film a few years ago called *Westworld* starring Yul Brynner, in which people could spend their holidays in a reconstruction of the old West. There were wonderfully realistic robot gunslingers for the customers to pit themselves against and, of course, shoot down. The 'dead' gunslingers were simply repaired in the workshop overnight and put back on the streets next morning. All this will be perfectly possible.

Eating out will also become a more regular feature of our lives. Like theme holidays, theme restaurants will be very popular – Roman banquets, Mexican fiestas, Victorian music halls, you name it. And we won't be eating food pills. Instead we will be taking for granted the vast variety of foodstuffs from all over the world that are available in specialist shops now.

The most dramatic breakthroughs in food production won't affect us in this country that much, but they will make a phenomenal difference to the Third World. New genetic engineering techniques will be able to produce, literally overnight, new strains of cereals – wheat, rice, and so on. These will grow faster, produce bigger yields and be disease-resistant, a process that previously took many years of selective cultivation.

All this leisure time spent holidaying and eating sounds like very hard work, so will we be fit enough to cope? There will be vaccines against killer diseases like malaria, techniques to conquer hereditary diseases. Work is already under way on finding a synthetic material to make organs for transplantation which won't be rejected by the body. And diabetes will certainly be much simpler to control. Sufferers may have minute sensors and pumps implanted in their bodies which automatically adjust the insulin level in the blood.

There will also be manned space stations with 10 or 15 astronauts at most carrying out research. And we may know whether there are other forms of intelligent life in space because there will be a radio-observatory on the far side of the moon. It will be permanently shielded from the constant stream of radio chattering coming up from the earth, so it will be able to pick up any faint signals from deep space.

Cars will still be with us, although their body panels will probably be plastic so that you can click on new ones, like Lego, when they're damaged (they won't rust, of course) or when you get bored with the colour or the style. They'll have on-board computers that will not only tell you how efficiently you're driving, but can tell you just exactly what's going wrong with the car. And they could be powered by anything from electricity to methane gas.

When you think about the future, it's worth remembering that progress has never moved in a straight logical line, and that history is littered with sudden developments that no one could have foreseen. Take the early American futurologist who predicted in the 1850s that if the horse traffic in New York went on increasing at the same rate, by 1950 the streets would be six feet deep in manure! What he couldn't have known then was that an invention called the motor car was just around the corner.

Questions

1 Explain in your own words the type of holidays which will be popular in the twenty-first century.
2 What will be special about the new types of cereals developed?
3 What three developments does the author say will make us fitter?
4 How will we be able to know whether there are other forms of intelligent life in space?
5 Suggest a suitable title for this passage and give reasons for your choice.
6 What do *you* think life will be like in the twenty-first century?
7 The writer describes a prediction about horse manure. What point is he trying to illustrate?

COFFEE? BREAK - IRELAND

RUSH HOUR-IRELAND

1   Look carefully at these two postcards. What ideas are being conveyed in each card?
2   Do you agree with the image of Ireland portrayed in these cards? Give reasons.
3   Imagine that you are a journalist working for Bord Fáilte. Write two paragraphs encouraging tourists to holiday in Ireland.

It doesn't cook, clean, cut, polish, sew, steam, wash, dry, iron, blend, mend or mash.

(But it's the most powerful appliance in the home.)

In almost every house in Ireland you'll find a television. And watching RTE on TV are almost two million people every day. Only RTE can deliver such massive audiences - covering every single market sector - on a daily basis. If you want your advertising to really hit home, switch on to the power of RTE television.

C O M P E L L I N G   S E L L I N G

1   In what type of publication would you expect to find this advertisement? Why?

2   The artist focuses your attention on the box. Why do you think she does this?

3   Which aspect of the advertisement do you feel is the most important? Explain why.

4   Statistics show that people are strongly influenced by television advertising. What are your thoughts on the subject?

▶ **Reynard the Fox**

The fox was strong, he was full of running,
He could run for an hour and then be cunning,
But the cry behind him made him chill,
They were nearer now and they meant to kill.
They meant to run him until his blood
Clogged on his heart as his brush with mud,
Till his back bent up and his tongue hung flagging,

And his belly and brush were filthed from dragging,
Till he crouched stone-still, dead-beat and dirty,
With nothing but teeth against the thirty.
And all the way to that blinding end
He would meet with men and have none his friend:
Men to holloa and men to run him,
With stones to stagger and yells to stun him
Men to head him with whips to beat him,
Teeth to mangle and mouths to eat him.
And all the way, that wild high crying,
To hold his blood with the thought of dying,
The horn and the cheer, and the dream-like thunder
Of the horsehooves stamping the meadows under.

And here, as he ran to the huntsman's yelling,
The fox first felt that the pace was telling;
His body and lungs seemed all grown old,
His legs less certain, his heart less bold,
The hound-noise nearer, the hill-slope steeper,
The thud in the blood of his body deeper,
His pride in his speed, his joy in the race,
Were withered away, for what use was pace?
He had run his best, and the hounds ran better,
Then the going worsened, the earth was wetter.
Then his brush drooped down till it sometimes dragged,
And his fur felt sick and his chest was tagged
With taggles of mud, and his pads seemed lead,
It was well for him he'd an earth ahead.

John Masefield

Questions

1 What, in your opinion, was *John Masefield's* intention in writing this poem?
2 What emotions does the poem arouse in you?
3 Did the fox in the poem escape? Give reasons for your answer.
4 The pace of the poem is rather brisk in the beginning. Why does this pace slow down as the poem progresses?
5 The poem is rich in descriptive images. Select some examples which appeal to you and give reasons for your choice.

PERSONAL AND FUNCTIONAL WRITING

1 You have just returned home from an exchange holiday to France. Unfortunately you have forgotten your walkman. Write a **postcard** to the French family thanking them for their hospitality and asking them to forward your personal stereo.

2 Write a short **newspaper article** based on the following guidelines. Cork – St Paul's College – Friday – lunch break – telephone call – bomb alert – canteen area – students evacuated – building searched – a practical joke.

3 Write a **composition** on one of the following titles.
(a) Advertisements
(b) Walking in the country
(c) Annoying habits
(d) The perfect holiday

1 Make a list of the common nouns contained in the following sentences:
   The young child threw pebbles and stones into the water.
   Thirty years ago farmers sold their animals at the fair.
   The young girl wrote a letter to her favourite aunt.
   A stream of blood was pouring from the boy's knee.

2 Correct one error in each of the following:
   (a) They should have went last week.
   (b) She has forgot the name of the shop.
   (c) The weather has being very cold.

3 Punctuate the following passage:
   if my dad wins the grand prix said mark hell visit france spain and
   germany before april and he promised that hed bring me with him on the
   tour

4 Spelling test

neglect	weary	truth	cruelty	breathe
imitate	fierce	civilise	anxious	friendship
faith	quarrel	mischief	occasion	athlete
relieve	loose	lose	encourage	advertise

UNIT 16

READING

➤ Mr Dobbs Retires

I saw Dobbs for the first time that summer evening when I turned the corner of the street that led to the Works Gate. We were both due on shift work at ten o'clock and already we were late. He was about thirty yards ahead of me, an undersized man with his supper in a parcel under one arm, and he was standing quite still. That surprised me, I remember, because Dobbs was one of the most meticulous timekeepers on the job. I stopped too, not wanting to pass him. It was a wide, dusty street, quite deserted at that late hour, with a summer peace over it that comes even to the dockside when the wagons and the floats have drawn their last loads and called it a day. There was discarded cigarette cartons lying here and there in the channel. They had curled up throughout the heat of the long day. I can remember the sky above the works glowing with red and gold and, outlined against it, the great chimneys sending up their steady black smoke.

Dobbs had his head a little to one side, listening for something. After a while it came – a rumbling sound, distant at first, which grew and grew until the street was full of it, and then slowly receded. It was the Wexford mail, thundering southwards. I thought of my father in the little cottage by the railway line and knew he was going over to the kitchen dresser to check the alarm clock by it. He was a shift worker too, and he had been doing that as long as I could remember. That evening the thought made me sad, because any day now I'd be leaving him to try my luck somewhere else. Three weeks as a trainee with Dobbs had convinced me that there were better things in life than playing nursemaid to a conveyor belt from ten at night to six in the morning. I loved my father, I suppose, but I was twenty-three at the time, an age when summer skies make promises they don't always keep.

Dobbs was already at the time office, talking to the gateman, when I took my card from the rack and put it in the clock.

'Fifty years I'm in it,' he was saying in a voice that was not quite his own.

I remembered then that he was being retired the following day. It was his last night on shift work. The clock made a tiny ping of sound when I pressed the lever but neither of them noticed – they had heard it too often. I lit a cigarette and began to listen, my hands in my pockets, my eyes looking down the works yard, where the telfer, suspended from its rail, was making a slow and graceful parabola high above us.

'It isn't long going over,' I heard the gateman say. He sighed. He was an old man too.

'Not in the heel of the hunt,' Dobbs answered.

'Still,' said the gateman, 'it'll be good to be finished with the shift work. You'll be able to get into bed at night and up in the morning for a change. That's a hell of a lot better than vice versa.'

'More Christian anyway,' Dobbs said.

'More natural altogether,' the gateman insisted, and I could hear they were both trying hard to be cheerful about it, to be cheerful about the fact that time passed and years ran out all too quickly.

 **uestions**

1 Why was Dobbs carrying a parcel, which contained his supper, under his arm?
2 Why was the narrator sad on that particular evening?
3 Why do you think the writer chose to use the following words:
— meticulous
— thundering
— nursemaid
4 What do you think the writer meant by the line:
'An age when summer skies make promises they don't always keep'.
5 From the evidence of the extract what type of person do you imagine Dobbs to be?
6 Why do you think Dobbs was listening for the Wexford Mail train on that particular evening?
7 What type of work were the men doing in your opinion? Give reasons.
8 Write a short dialogue between Dobbs and the young man to illustrate the theme of the extract as you see it.

- Give the title and author of a **novel** or a **play** you have studied in which one of the main parts is played by a boy or a girl.
- Write a brief account of the part played by the young person.
- Name one other character in the novel or play whom you liked or disliked. Give reasons for your choice.

PERSONAL AND FUNCTIONAL WRITING

1 As headmaster or headmistress of a second level college, write a **letter** to the parents of an expelled pupil. Explain your reasons for the expulsion.

2 You are a journalist reporting from the scene of a recent earthquake. Write a **report** for your newspaper in which you describe the earthquake as it happened and the horrific scenes in the aftermath of the quake.

3 Write a **composition** on one of the following titles:
   (a) Pocket money   (c) What I like and dislike about school
   (b) A prison escape   (d) Hijacked.

GRAMMAR

1 Re-arrange the following words into pairs with similar meanings:

vacant	deceive	surrender	quick
steed	apart	asunder	horse
rough	yield	cheat	foe
sleek	valour	bravery	smooth
enemy	empty	prompt	coarse

2 Punctuate the following passage:
can i help you yes please i am looking for dr kelly the doctor is not here at the moment when he comes back would you tell him that mr ryan of church street has had an accident and needs a doctor quickly very well i wont forget

3 Write the abstract nouns which are formed from the following words.

happy	poor	curious	strong	generous
lazy	angry	careless	jealous	brave

4 Put apostrophes in the following sentences, where these are necessary:
Johns books are in his fathers desk. This is a boys school. The girls school is a mile away. Whos afraid of the big bad wolf? Theres no money in the till. Whats that boy doing? Mr Kellys dog is missing. He sells mens overcoats. When youre ready, well go for a walk to Marys house. Lets go home.

5 Change each of the following sentences to reported speech:
'I am not going to punish you,' the teacher told me,
'What have you done with the money?' my father asked me.
'I will go to the cinema tomorrow,' John told his mother.
'The bus is full; you will have to wait for the next,' the conductor told my sister.

1   Suggest a suitable title for this picture and give reasons for your choice.
2   What would your next action be if you were the driver of the tractor?
3   Imagine what the pilot was thinking in the moment captured by the
    camera. Write four sentences which express his thoughts.
4   This plane crash actually happened. The photograph was taken by an
    amateur photographer. Summarise the crash in a paragraph for inclusion
    in the RTE 9.00 pm news bulletin.

urban survival

RESPRO bandit™
ANTI POLLUTION SCARF

other colours: ◆ blue
◆ grey
☠ black

The Respro® Bandit™ combines a <u>washable</u> activated charcoal cloth normally reserved for bacterial and chemical warfare protection with a scarf made from 100% cotton. So... if you want a total package of at least <u>six</u> months protection against urban pollution for around £10.00 then call us now.

PROTECTION FACTOR

Petrol fumes
Diesel fumes
Low level ozone
Acid gases
Lead oxide
Pollen
Irritant dusts

**INFORMATION LINE
071 721 7300**

RESPRO®
PRODUCTS... MADE IN THE UK

1 Read the text of this advertisement and say (a) how much of the advertisement is information and (b) how much is persuasion.
2 What is the purpose of the photograph which accompanies the copy?
3 What features of this advertisement are designed to capture the readers' attention? What needs and desires are appealed to?
4 There is an obvious play on words. Give examples of this and say how effective this technique is.

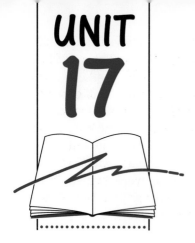

READING

➤ Operation 'Mincemeat'

It was 1943. After three and a half years of war, the Allies (Britain and America) were ready at last to invade occupied Europe and try to recapture it from the Germans. The Allied Commanders believed that the best place from which to launch the attack was the island of Sicily, off the southern tip of Italy. However, they also suspected that Germany would expect the attack to come from there and would defend the Sicilian beaches as heavily as they could. British Intelligence officers racked their brains for a way round the problem. Would it be possible to trick the Germans into thinking that the invasion would come from somewhere else? Could false information be fed to German Intelligence in such a way that they would believe it? And if so, what sort of a messenger could be relied upon to carry out such a vital but dangerous mission? No agent alive could be expected to convince German Intelligence of such a thing... unless... Slowly a daring and dramatic plan began to form in the minds of British Intelligence officers: they *would* send a false message by a British agent; but the agent would be a corpse... 'Operation Mincemeat' was born.

Once they had decided on their bold plan of action, British Intelligence worked quickly. First of all, they obtained the body of a young man who had died of pneumonia, and dressed it in the uniform of an officer in the Royal Marines. Then they faked papers to indicate that this man was a British agent carrying top secret information about the Allied landings. Carefully they made it clear in the papers that the landings would be made in Greece and Sardinia, *not* Sicily. These papers were put in a briefcase which was attached to the corpse's wrist.

But British Intelligence didn't stop there. Their 'messenger' had to appear to be a real person if he was to convince the enemy, and so the officers set about creating a whole new identity for him. They named him 'Major Martin' and forged an identity card for him compete with a convincing photograph and some well-read love letters from an imaginary girl-friend. Letters from a cross bank manager and a rather stuck-up father were added. His wallet was filled with these and with lots of other bits of this and that such as people so often carry about with them. As a final touch, the officers even thought of entering the notice of 'Major Martin's' death in the columns of *The Times* newspaper.

Now came the last part: the test of all their planning and work. With great secrecy British Intelligence shipped the body to Southern Spain and slipped it into the sea from a submerged submarine, hoping that it would wash up on a beach near Huelva – a town in which German agents were known to be operating. And with 'Major Martin' launched on his lonely mission, the officers who had sent him could only sit back and wait and hope. Would the papers be found, and would German High Command be convinced?

They needn't have worried. 'Operation Mincemeat' went according to plan. The body was found and the fake information reported, investigated and accepted by Hitler himself. Orders were given to the German army to move men and guns from Sicily to Greece and Sardinia, leaving a much clearer path for the Allied landings. 'Major Martin', 'the man who never was', had pulled off one of the most extraordinary and successful operations of the Second World War.

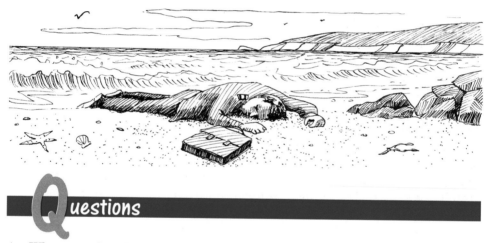

Questions

1 Why were the Allies anxious to feed false information to the Germans?
2 What steps did British Intelligence take to make the plan convincing?
3 Why was the body shipped to Southern Spain?
4 Do you think that Operation Mincemeat was an appropriate name for the plan?
5 What evidence is there in the story to suggest that the Allies were one step ahead of the Germans?
6 Which element in the plan do you think was the most important? Why?
7 Why do you think the Allies wanted to land in Sicily rather than Greece or Sardinia?
8 Imagine that Adolf Hitler had discovered the truth about Major Martin. How do you think he would have dealt with the situation?

➤ The Ballad of Father Gilligan

The old priest Peter Gilligan
Was weary night and day;
For half his flock were in their beds,
Or under green sods lay.

Once, while he nodded on a chair,
At the moth-hour of eve,
Another poor man sent for him,
And he began to grieve.

'I have no rest, nor joys, nor peace,
For people die and die',
And after cried he, 'God forgive!
My body spake, not I.'

He knelt, and leaning on the chair
He prayed and fell asleep;
And the moth-hour went from the fields,
And stars began to peep.

They slowly into millions grew,
And leaves shook in the wind;
And God covered the world with shade,
And whispered to mankind.

Upon the time of sparrow-chirp
When moths came once more,
The old priest Peter Gilligan
Stood upright on the floor.

'Mavrone, mavrone! the man has died
While I slept on the chair';
He roused his horse out of its sleep,
And rode with little care.

He rode now as he never rode,
By rocky lane and fen;
The sick man's wife opened the door:
'Father! you come again!'

'And is the poor man dead?' he cried.
'He died an hour ago.'
The old priest Peter Gilligan
In grief swayed to and fro.

'When you were gone, he turned and died
As merry as a bird.'
The old priest Peter Gilligan
He knelt him at that word.

'He Who hath made the night of stars
For souls who tire and bleed,
Sent one of His great angels down
To help me in my need.'

'He Who is wrapped in purple robes,
With planets in His care,
Had pity on the least of things.
Asleep upon a chair.'

W. B. Yeats

Questions

1 Summarise briefly the story of this poem by *W.B. Yeats.*
2 When do you think the events may have taken place? Give your reasons.
3 What features of the poem show that it is a ballad?
4 Pick out a number of images or phrases from the poem which you like.
   Explain why you chose them.
5 What feelings are you left with at the end of the poem?

1   Write a **letter** to a close friend persuading him/her to take up some leisure activity which already gives you a good deal of pleasure.

2   Write a **short story** beginning with the words:
    'Don't tell me you forgot the matches'.

3   Write a **composition** on one of the following titles:
    (a) Visiting the dentist
    (b) Summer jobs
    (c) Unusual hobbies
    (d) Planning for the future.

GRAMMAR

1   Form verbs from the following abstract nouns:

choice	length
belief	friendship
recognition	variety
width	dampness
success	disobedience

2   Correct one error in each of the following:
    (a) The referee said that it was a fowl.
    (b) Michael taught that he would win.
    (c) The copies were laying on the desk.

3   Punctuate the following passage:
    can you tell me where i can find the post office if you turn right at the next crossing you will be in main street and the post office is in the middle of the street what time does it close half past five

4   Change each of the following sentences to reported speech:
    'The new park will be opened next Sunday,' said the mayor.
    'We will be going to France on holidays next summer,' my father promised.
    'I was swimming in the river yesterday,' Michael informed me.
    'You will have to work harder in school,' the teacher said to me.

5   Complete each of the following sentences by using *who, which, that* or *whom*:
    There is the girl ____ lost the books.
    She has a dog ____ barks at strangers.
    A woman to ____ I was speaking told me.
    He does not like the painting ____ hangs in the hall.
    We followed the path ____ leads to the village.
    The man ____ I saw was a burglar.

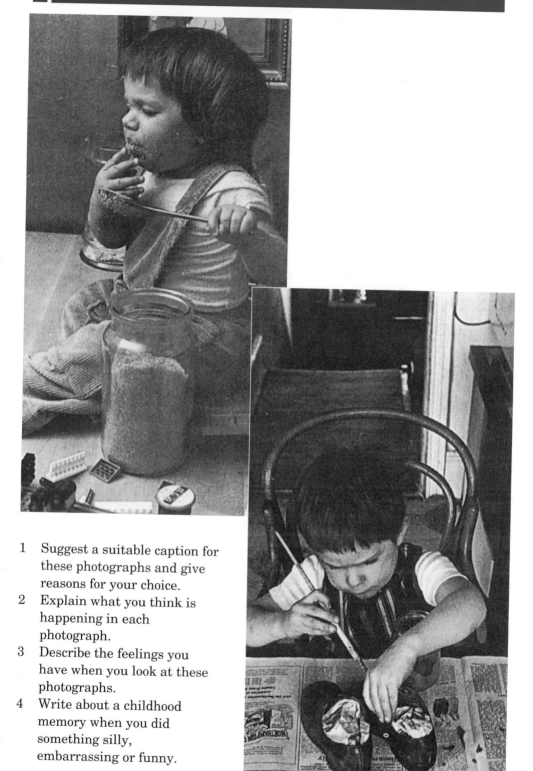

1 Suggest a suitable caption for these photographs and give reasons for your choice.
2 Explain what you think is happening in each photograph.
3 Describe the feelings you have when you look at these photographs.
4 Write about a childhood memory when you did something silly, embarrassing or funny.

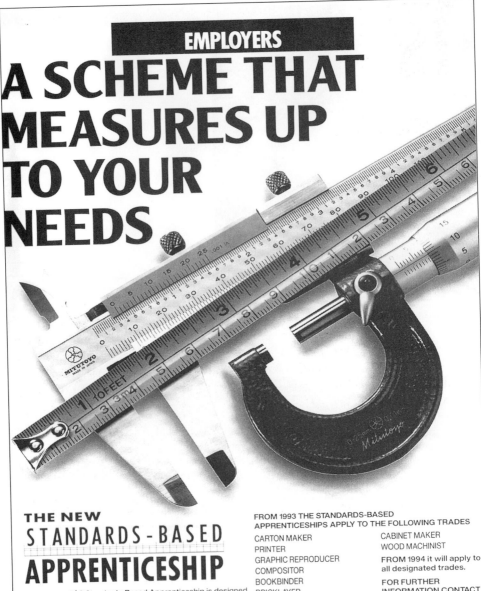

EMPLOYERS

A SCHEME THAT MEASURES UP TO YOUR NEEDS

THE NEW
STANDARDS-BASED
APPRENTICESHIP

The new FÁS Standards-Based Apprenticeship is designed to help apprentices measure up to your particular needs.

It is based on uniform, pre-specified and industry-agreed standards derived from the current and future requirements of Irish industry.

On successful completion of the new apprenticeship, apprentices will receive a National Craft Certificate. This nationally and internationally recognised certificate will enhance the reputation of Irish companies employing craftspersons.

FROM 1993 THE STANDARDS-BASED APPRENTICESHIPS APPLY TO THE FOLLOWING TRADES

CARTON MAKER
PRINTER
GRAPHIC REPRODUCER
COMPOSITOR
BOOKBINDER
BRICKLAYER
PLASTERER
PAINTER/DECORATOR
VEHICLE BODY REPAIRER
AGRICULTURAL MECHANIC
AIRCRAFT MECHANIC
REFRIGERATION CRAFTSPERSON
SHEET METAL WORKER

CABINET MAKER
WOOD MACHINIST

FROM 1994 it will apply to all designated trades.

FOR FURTHER INFORMATION CONTACT YOUR LOCAL FÁS OFFICE.

1. Any advertisement has a target audience in mind. At whom is this advertisement aimed?
2. Suggest reasons why the advertisement contains several print sizes.
3. Why do you think the props in this advertisement were chosen?
4. What in your opinion, is the key phrase in this advertisement?

READING

➤ Arctic search

'We haven't any covers, but you can curl around that stone,' said Kayak. 'Be careful not to touch it. Stones are cold unless they're in the sun. Just curl around it to protect your body from the wind. Then if the wind shifts, you shift too, so the wind's full strength won't hit you. It's a woman's trick my mother taught me. It's a good way to sleep out on the land when you got no sleeping skins with you. Put your parka on backwards, Mattoosie, the way I'm doing it, and pull your arms inside, out of your sleeves, and hug your body,' Kayak said. 'Now pull your hood up over your face and let your breath go down around your body. It will help to keep you warm. If you get too cold, your feet will wake you up. Then you get to jump up and run and flap your arms like a duck till you feel warm again.'

Matthew bedded down around the stone as he was told and within a few minutes both boys were sleeping soundly, so soundly they did not hear the thunking of Matilda's noisy, whirling blades as the helicopter flew in towards their distant camp.

When Matthew awoke, he felt a chill on his left side seeping up from the cold ground and yet his right side was heated by the by-now strong yellow sunlight of the Arctic morning. He saw Kayak quickly reverse his parka. He pulled a small package of raisins and two large hardtack biscuits from their pack. They shared these and drank cold clear water from a pond.

'If my Mom were here,' said Matthew, 'she'd say, 'Sonny, brush your teeth.''

'Mattoosie, you could go back to our tents, if you want to,' Kayak said. 'You just follow the fox traps. They will lead you to camp. I'm going right now and try to find the wild man. We brought your father and Charlie out here by promising we would show them gold. But we can't find it. The wild man's the only one who knows exactly where it is.'

Matthew looked back over the rolling tundra country with snow still clinging to the north sides of the hills. He was not at all sure he *could* find his way to their small red tents.

'No, I'll come with you,' he said. 'But we've got to hurry. We should have left a note for Dad and Charlie so they wouldn't worry.'

Kayak was already on his feet and moving fast to warm himself, heading into the north, following the wild man's trail.

It was nearly noon, when they came to a huge crack in the granite ridge they were following. The crack was filled with solid ice.

'I've heard about that kind of frozen place,' Kayak said as he pointed to the ice fault between the two steep walls of granite. 'but I never thought I'd see one. My father told me that the ice hardly melts at all in one of these,' said Kayak. 'It's so strong and thick and old and shaded by the stone cliffs on either side that it just stays like that, only dripping a little bit in summer. Then winter comes and builds it up and makes it hard as flint again.'

'It looks like a small glacier,' said Matt. 'My father would call it a fissure.'

Kayak studied the ice fault carefully. 'It's no good to try and cross it here. We'll have to go to that narrow place.' He pointed at a faint crushed trail in the tundra.

Matt nodded in agreement.

'I think that's what the wild man did,' said Kayak.

They walked along the edge of the cliff until they came to a narrow path with well-worn stepping places that led down the glacial ice fault.

Cautiously, they moved forward, ducked under an ice ledge and found themselves inside a hollow cave. It was not very cold, but everything was wrapped in blue-green shadows. Sharp icicles hung from the roof of the cave. Water dripped steadily from them like the tick-tick-ticking of some ancient clock.

'This place makes me a little nervous,' Matthew whispered.

'Me, too,' said Kayak. 'I never saw an ice cave like this before in all my life. This is the kind of hidden den where Igtuk the boomer lives. That's what my grandmother told us when we were listening to the winter stories.'

'Who's Igtuk the boomer?' Matthew asked him.

'He's a mountain spirit who causes ice slides. He goes *'Igk-Igk-Igk'*, until the awful sound is so loud it breaks your ears right off your head.'

'You don't believe that, do you?' Matthew whispered.

'When I'm sitting in school at Frobisher,' Kayak whispered back, 'I don't believe it and I laugh about those old grandfather stories with most of the other kids. But now that I'm down inside this ice cave, well... I believe in Igtuk. How about you?'

'It's hard not to,' Matthew said, and shivered. 'Down here I believe in everything.' His words echoed, *Thing – thing – thing.*

'Talk softly,' Kayak shuddered. 'I hate the way our voices echo.' *Echo-echo!* 'It makes these ice walls seem to answer.' *Answer-answer!*

Together, step by step, they crept deeper and deeper into the frightening, crouching shadows of the cave. The cold ice passage seemed to go on forever.

'It's got to end somewhere,' Kayak said at last. *Where – where -where!*

'I wish we'd brought the flashlight,' Matthew whispered.

At that very moment, something spun down and hit him a stunning blow on the head. Even as he fell, he saw Kayak go crashing down also. The awful sound of high-pitched, crazy laughter echoed through the blue ice cave.

Questions

1 Explain in your own words how the two boys survived the cold night.
2 How would Matthew know if he got too cold during the night?
3 Why was Kayak searching for the wild man?
4 Who do you think is producing the crazy laughter at the end of the extract?
5 From the evidence of the extract, what type of person do you imagine the wild man to be?
6 Why do you think the writer chose to use the following words:
   - whirling
   - flint
   - tundra
   - cautiously
7 List as many pieces of information as you can find to show that the events in this extract take place in modern times.
8 How does this story make you feel?
9 What do you think happened next? Explain your answer.

WHAT I HAVE READ

- It has been said that a good poem is like a picture or a painting. Choose a **poem** that you have studied which you feel meets this description.
- Give the story of the poem in your own words, quoting freely from the poem.
- Write a brief note explaining why the poem you have chosen appeals to you

PERSONAL AND FUNCTIONAL WRITING

1 After purchasing an expensive cassette or CD system you discover that it is faulty. Write a **letter** of complaint to the shopkeeper asking for a refund or a replacement.

2 A world famous celebrity has recently visited your area. Write a **report** for your school magazine giving details of the visit and try to describe the atmosphere of the locality during the event.

3 Write a **composition** on one of the following titles:
   (a) Grown-ups do not understand children.
   (b) A frightening nightmare
   (c) Homework
   (d) Moving house

NOBODY OFFERS YOU A BETTER COACH SERVICE

Dublin

express

BUS

Return fares from Dublin

WATERFORD	£8.00
ROSSLARE	£10.00
BALLINA	£11.00
SLIGO	£11.00
BELFAST	£12.00
ENNIS	£12.00
GALWAY	£12.00
LIMERICK	£12.00
DONEGAL	£13.00
LETTERKENNY	£13.00
CORK	£15.00
TRALEE	£17.00

Travel mid-week at bargain return fares. Ask for details.

Something for Everyone

Take a Day Tour From as Little as £10
Take the family out for a great day on one of our day tours. Choose from over 60 tours nationwide. From as little as £10 per person. Ask for our DAY TOURS brochure.

Mini Breaks for £33
Our BREAKAWAY brochure shows you how to get away from it all. A choice of 24 locations. Terrific value at £33 per night sharing. Includes overnight accommodation, full Irish breakfast and return coach fare to your choice of destination.

Travel in Style. You'll enjoy the comfort and luxury of our award winning coaches. They're superb.

For travel information ring:
Central Bus Station (Busaras), Store Street, Dublin 1. (01) 366111.
Parnell Place Bus Station, Cork. (021) 508188.
Colbert Station, Limerick. (061) 313333.
Ceannt Station, Galway. (091) 62000.
Plunkett Station, Waterford. (051) 79000.
Casement Station, Tralee. (066) 23566.
Or your local Bus Éireann Office, Tourist Office, or Travel Agent.

BUS ÉIREANN
we're on the move

1 What overall message does this advertisement intend to convey?
2 What is the focus of attention in the advertisement?
3 How significant is the company logo in this advertisement? Give reasons.
4 Statistics prove that people are strongly influenced by media advertising. What are the advantages and disadvantages for the consumer?

1 Suggest a suitable title for this picture and give reasons for your choice.
2 How would you describe the young boy's expression?
3 Where do you think this picture was taken? Why?
4 Write a short dialogue between a passerby and the young boy as he sits on
   the path.

GRAMMAR

1 Punctuate the following passage:
   where do you think youre going with that bicycle shouted sergeant kelly im
   late for the bus replied the thief and ive urgent business in town you have
   indeed said the sergeant justice byrne is very anxious to meet you

2 Write out this list of words in your copy with the correct words in the
   spaces:

I give	I gave	I have given
I bring	_____	_____
I begin	_____	_____
I know	_____	_____
I go	_____	_____
I make	_____	_____
I ring	_____	_____
I shake	_____	_____
I fall	_____	_____

3 Make a list of the proper nouns contained in the following sentences:
   Mr Shaw said that France and Spain are neighbours.
   Every Friday John goes to Galway on the train.
   Robert and his friend sailed the Atlantic at Easter.
   For Christmas, Jane received a pet poodle called Rusty.

UNIT 19

NEWSPAPER REPORTING

In general, newspapers are divided into two main categories:

1. **Tabloid Newspapers**

   They are sometimes called 'Popular' newspapers and use the small page format.

   The Star and *The Sunday World* are two examples of this type of newspaper.

2. **Broadsheet Newspapers**

   They are sometimes called 'quality' newspapers and use the large page format.

   The Irish Times and *The Sunday Press* are two examples of this type of newspaper.

Tabloid and Broadsheet newspapers use very different styles of news reporting.

The following guidelines may help you to understand these differences more clearly.

Tabloid Newspapers	Broadsheet Newspapers
Sensational Headlines	More objective reporting
Some exaggeration	Balanced comment
Greater use of pictures	More text
Shorter sentences	Longer sentences
Emotive language	More formal style
Less balanced comment	

➤ **Two Versions**

Read carefully the following two reports of the same event taken from different newspapers and answer the questions asked.

PRESIDENT BUOYANT WITH OPTIMISM

Mary Robinson predicts a bright future for the whole of the Emerald Isle.

Ireland's First Lady was in a buoyant mood when interviewed in Atlanta during her recent visit to the United States.

She declared that she was overjoyed with recent developments in Northern Ireland and felt confident that the country would rapidly reach its full potential now that there was a lasting peace.

During the interview ·for American News Channel C.N.N., President Robinson referred to 'the great goodwill that exists on all sides' to find a lasting solution to the nightmare situation which has existed in Northern Ireland for more than a quarter of a century.

The vital ingredients of this news era must be contact, co-operation and respect for all, regardless of political tradition or religious belief.

She went on to warmly applaud the great interest taken by the United States and repeatedly stressed the vital importance of American support for the peace process.

President pleased with developments

The President, Mrs Robinson, said last night that she was 'very pleased' about recent developments in Ireland and believed they had brought about 'a shift in consciousness' on the island.

'There is a sense of the great possibilities that can emerge now that there has been a cessation of violence by the paramilitaries on both sides...A sense of moving to realise the full potential of the island of Ireland, building on the links of friendship already there."

In an interview on CNN television from Atlanta in the US, where she is on a visit, Mrs Robinson spoke of 'the great goodwill on all sides' to find a resolution to the problems of the North and of the 'buoyant mood' prevailing. She talked of the growing co-operation between businessmen, and tourism interests in particular.

Mrs Robinson said that from the beginning of her presidency she had wanted 'to encourage real friendship on the island of Ireland'. She spoke of her visits to the North and how various Northern groups continued to visit her in the Republic. It was important for people to make contact, she said, 'to break down barriers, to welcome pluralism and diversity, to get to know each other better, and have a sense of understanding'. This, she felt, was now 'happening by the week, strengthening by the month'. In all of this, she believed the support of the US and the EU was 'very important'.

1. How do the reports differ in their versions of the events?
2. What style of language is used in each report?
3. Comment on the headline used in each report.
4. Which report do you find the more interesting? Why?
5. From the following list, choose the most appropriate adjectives to describe each report:
   FACTUAL; INFORMATIVE; SENSATIONAL; BIASED; INACCURATE; COLD; SUGGESTIVE; INTIMATE; CLICHED; ILLOGICAL.

UNIT 20

A CURRICULUM VITAE

When applying for a position you will probably have to include a Curriculum Vitae with your letter of application.

A good C.V. must always be properly typed, signed and dated. It should also include the following information.

Personal details: Name, address, telephone number, date of birth

Details of education: Schools attended, dates, subjects studied, examination results, qualifications obtained.

School interests: Teams, competitions, debates

Outside interests: Clubs, hobbies, charitable work.

Work experience: Work done outside of school, including dates and addresses of employers.

Present occupation: Address and brief description.

Other relevant information: Any worthwhile details not already listed.

Referees: The names and addresses of two people who are prepared to supply a reference for you.

Name: _____

Address _____
_____
_____

Telephone: _____

Date of birth: _____

Education: _____
Primary: _____
Dates _____

Post-Primary: _____
Dates: _____
Subjects: _____

Examination results:
a. Junior Certificate _____   b.   Leaving Certificate _____
_____   _____
_____   _____

Third-level College or **University**: _____
Dates: _____

Degree or other qualifications: _____

School Interests: _____

Outside interests: _____

Work Experience: _____
Dates: _____
Names and addresses of Employers: _____
Duties: _____

Present Occupation: _____
Address _____
Brief description: _____

Other relevant information: _____

Referees: _____
1. Name: Address _____

2. Name: Address _____

168

UNIT 21

LETTERS

- A good business letter must be clearly written in simple language.
- Short sentences should be used and all irrelevant material must be avoided.
- Even when writing a letter of complaint, the tone should be polite.
- The layout on the next page should be followed when writing this type of letter.

❏ FORMAL OPENINGS

Dear Mr/Mrs/Miss/Ms Kelly
Dear Sir
Dear Madam
Dear Sir or Madam

❏ FORMAL ENDING

Yours faithfully
Yours sincerely
Yours truly

Note: If you write to a particular person, you should end the letter 'Yours sincerely'.
        If the letter begins 'Dear Sir/Madam', you should end the letter 'Yours faithfully'.

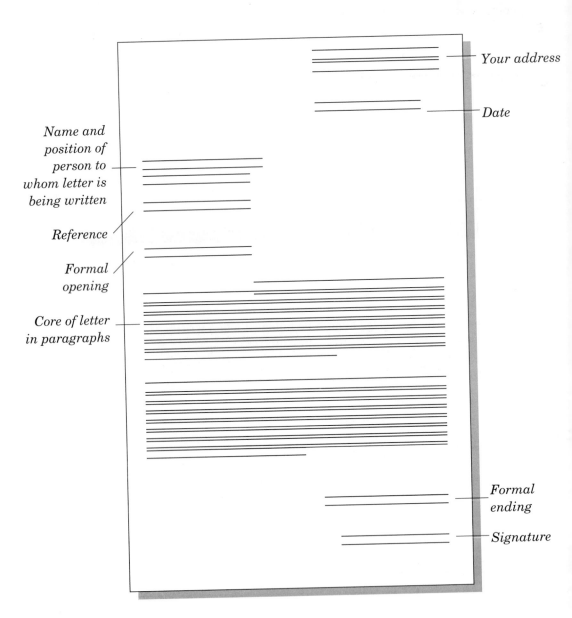

Your address

Date

Name and
position of
person to
whom letter is
being written

Reference

Formal
opening

Core of letter
in paragraphs

Formal
ending

Signature

- A personal letter is far less formal in style than a business letter.
- The language used depends on the relationship between the writer and the person to whom the letter is being written.
- The layout below should be followed when writing an informal, personal letter.

❑ PERSONAL LETTERS USUALLY END WITH

Yours Sincerely
All good wishes
Love

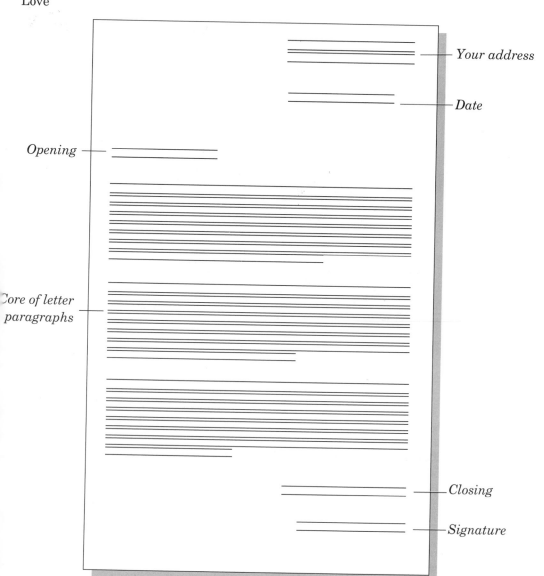

The layout of a letter to the editor (letter to a newspaper) is different from a business or personal letter.

You should begin with 'Sir' and end with 'Yours etc."

The style of this type of letter is usually semi-formal.

Here are two published examples of letters to the editor:

Lottery funds

Sir, – The reported drop in Lottery income share-out, as reported in the Dáil should be of concern to everyone.

In 1992, the total income was £252.3 million, of which £100.1 million was distributed to health, arts, sports and the Irish language. Yet in 1993, despite the total income increasing to £271.2 million, the amount distributed fell to £87.3 million.

In a speech given by John Major on September 16th to the English Heritage Conference, he estimated that between 1994 and 2001, no less than £9 billion will be distributed from the British National Lottery to heritage, sport, the arts, charities and the Millennium Fund. Even more interestingly, he promised that the British Government would not take advantage of the generation of so much money to cut its own spending programmes. Most significantly he went on to say: 'Let me emphasise that the money will not be under Government control. The distributing bodies will decide where the funds are spent'.

Such independence in terms of the decision-making process seems to me to be entirely appropriate. A similar system to the one outlined by John Major must be implemented in Ireland, as an immediate priority, if the Irish National Lottery is to continue to fulfil its original brief. – Yours, etc.

John O'Brien, Birr, Co. Offaly.

New Universities

Sir, – Like many others I welcome the cessation of violence in this part of the country. I also am aware that it will take a major effort by many to properly shape the future. For this reason I welcome the work being done by the Irish Government and others to get financial aid for the area. However, there is frequently a scarcity of good proposals for such assistance. I want to highlight one for Fermanagh that was first introduced to the public by John Hume, *i.e.* a new university campus.

The proposal, if implemented, would not alone benefit the county but would benefit the surrounding region which includes the counties of Donegal, Sligo, Leitrim, Cavan and Monaghan. Teachers, parents and young people in these counties are aware of the need for such an institution and would accept Enniskillen for its central location and other attractions compatible with academic life. – Yours, etc.,

Paul Kelly, Newpark, Enniskillen.